FOR BETTER, FOR WORSE

FOR BETTER, FOR WORSE

by

ELWYN ROBERTS

Printed by Gwasg y Bwthyn, Caernarfon

CONTENTS

TO

MY DAUGHTERS

LLINOS AND SIONED

WHO INSPIRED ME TO WRITE THIS BOOK

INTRODUCTION

It is my pleasure and privilege to introduce this book. *For Better, For Worse* will remind those of us who have known the Venerable Elwyn Roberts of the parts of life's journey that we have shared together. His thumbnail sketches of characters we have met in various parishes or committee meetings will let them smile upon us once more. We shall re-live the joys and frustrations of the Christian life experienced within the Church in Wales. Once again we shall appreciate the dignity and perceptiveness of Elwyn Roberts.

He was skilled in the art of resolving problems. After much discussion and debate Elwyn would reach for his briefcase, turn up the relevant section of the *Constitution of the Church in Wales* and produce the definitive answer. No wonder he was such an effective chairman, despite the occasions we could hardly see him behind the mountain of files on the diocesan registrar's desk.

There will also be many who have not known Elwyn Roberts personally who will enjoy reading this book. You will be given an insight into country life during the wartime years. You will learn a lot about the idiosyncrasies of the Church in Wales – its titles, characters, structures, activities – and have some of them explained. You will meet a parish priest and archdeacon who earned the respect and the affection of all his colleagues. Although he is writing his autobiography you will note his humility – not once does he blow his own trumpet. Most especially, you will be struck by Elwyn's courage as he continues his activities despite the onslaught of Parkinson's Disease nineteen years ago. He made a deliberate decision and kept to it: "There is no point in moaning about your lot – you just have to get on with it." Apart from the wonderful support of his family he had two gifts which enabled him to do this: a unique sense of humour that colours every page of this book and a deep spirituality summed up in the prayer that he quotes at the end. Therein lies the secret of Elwyn's proverbial wisdom and courage.

SAUNDERS DAVIES
Bishop of Bangor

PREFACE

This book is the result of a suggestion made by my family that it would be more profitable for me to do something more constructive with my life than watch television!

So I thought that I would give a picture of what a clergyman's life is all about. For 19 years though, the course of my life has been governed by Parkinson's Disease and that is why this is referred to so often. I do hope that what is said will give encouragement to other sufferers and their carers.

I am grateful to the following for making it possible to publish this book:

- Mr Maldwyn Thomas and the Staff of Gwasg Pantycelyn/ Gwasg y Bwthyn for their much appreciated advice and guidance.
- The Isla Johnston Trust for its generous contribution towards the cost of publication. I also wish to acknowledge another generous gift from a sponsor who wishes to remain anonymous.
- The Right Reverend Saunders Davies and Dr Enid Pierce Roberts who kindly offered, despite leading busy lives, to read the proofs.
- Above all, my wife, Eiflyn for transferring my hand written version into print, and for ensuring that my book sees the light of day. Without her help, all this would not have been possible.

I have included in the short Appendix some simple notes relating to the Church in Wales for the benefit of those who are not familiar with the workings of that Church.

ELWYN ROBERTS

Chapter 1

THE FAMILY

My father, John, was one of ten children born to John and Sarah Grace Roberts, Storws, Llanddona. What was kept in this Storws (Storehouse), situated on the edge of the sea in the northern corner of Red Wharf Bay, I don't know. The more romantic associated it with a place where smugglers stored their loot but more likely it was a place where fishermen stored their equipment. As this extensive beach was a potential landing strip for German invaders during the second World War, this expanse was broken up by poles (set at intervals in the sand) to prevent enemy aircraft landing. Further up, on the cliff top there was a gun emplacement disguised as a house to foil any attempted invasion from the sea. It was here that Mary the youngest of the Storws girls met Joe Rimmer, one of the gun crew whom she later married. What Taid Llanddona did for a living I don't know for certain but I have an idea that he worked at least for a time at the Penmon Quarry. Nain Llanddona I remember as a jovial, kindly and generous person.

My mother, Elin Myfanwy, was the younger daughter of Hugh Edward and Elizabeth Catherine Griffith of Holyhead. Taid Holyhead, of whom I have only vague childhood memories, appears to have been active in the life of the community and especially in the church where he was a Churchwarden for many years (no time limit for Churchwardens in those days!). He was a joiner by trade and worked on the Holyhead/Dublin boats. He was a skilled craftsman and many pieces of his handiwork are still treasured by the family, including an assortment of grandfather clocks. My recollections of him however, are rather scanty as he died at a comparatively early age.

I never knew Nain Holyhead at her best and her latter years were clouded by sadness. She nursed Taid through a long illness, when she scarcely left his bedside for months, and the experience of having 15 Newry Fawr, her home, hit by a German bomb, probably meant for the harbour, all took their toll and left her suffering from what we today would call senile dementia but that at a comparatively early age. This is a sad condition which affects not only the sufferer but also the whole family. When Nain could no longer fend for herself the two daughters, my mother and Auntie Mag, took it in turns to have Nain to stay at their homes. I vividly remember the air of gloom and foreboding we experienced as our turn to have Nain drew near, and the relief we felt when we had done our stint and it became time for Auntie Mag to have her. But this is to anticipate.

After attending school at Holyhead, my mother moved on to St Mary's College, Bangor, to train as a teacher, while my father attended Beaumaris Grammar School, walking there and back daily, which involved a journey of a distance of some five miles, including climbing a very steep hill from Storws to Llanddona village.

When the 1914 – 18 war broke out my father volunteered for military service, having made out that he was older than he was in order to be accepted. On discharge from the army (about which he spoke very little) he attended UCNW, Bangor, where he graduated and then proceeded to St Michael's Theological College, Llandaff, for theological training prior to ordination. He was ordained Deacon on St Matthew's Day 1923 to serve in the parish of Holyhead and he was priested a year later. Soon the new curate and the Churchwarden's daughter were married and John was appointed to a curacy at Llandudno where they set up their new home. There they remained until John was appointed to the incumbency of Pentir in 1930.

Chapter 2

EARLY YEARS

It was in Pentir Vicarage on 13th September 1931 that I was born and it was here that I spent the first eighteen years of my life. That almost proved to be a very short life, for at the age of six I was seriously ill with peritonitis and taken to the C.&A. Infirmary, (where Safeways is now), where I was operated on by Dr Ifan Huw Jones who was about to leave the hospital after a day's work but was called back to attend to me. Those were the pre-penicillin and antibiotic days and I'm told that when he called at the hospital the day following the operation, the Doctor had the shock of his life to find me still alive. They were also the days when it was not nursing practice to allow parents to visit their children in hospital, so I spent thirteen weeks in the C.&A. cut off from my family and friends.

The children's ward was on the upper floor of the wing overlooking the town and about the only toy we had to while away the time was an old wooden rocking horse. This was regularly commandeered by the ward bully – Gwynfor, and he is one of the less happy memories of the C.&A. One of the more pleasant memories was a young pupil nurse who in due course married Tom Bayley Hughes who later became my predecessor as Archdeacon of Bangor. By the time it came for me to go home I was completely institutionalised.

My brother Basil was also born at Pentir on 1st May 1935. The Vicarage was situated about half-way between the communities of Rhiwlas and Glasinfryn, both of which had a primary school, but as Glasinfryn was a 'Church School' the expectation was that the Vicar's children would attend there. So Glasinfryn it was. It was a two teacher school with Miss Hughes (later Mrs Roberts) in charge of the infants and the Headmaster, Huw Fon Roberts, in charge of the Senior classes.

Some snapshots spring to mind when thinking of the school – the daily walk of about two miles there and back in all weathers, writing on slates (yes, we still made some use of slates even in those days), open coal fire-places with milk bottles around the fire guard, warming up in cold weather. I also vividly remember the periodic visit of the Schools' Dentist with his primitive instruments which seemed more suitable to a medieval torture chamber. Of course there was no electric power so he had to use pedal power to work the drill! I also remember the games which came and went in due season – marbles, conkers, tick, the brown box with gas mask and woe betide anyone who forgot to bring it or mislaid it. Remember that there was a war on for much of our childhood years, and this influenced the games we played.

Glasinfryn was a happy school and I have grateful memories of the time I spent there. In many primary schools of the period the great thing was to achieve success in the 11 plus or Scholarship, and the quality of the Primary School was judged by its performance in this examination. But the scholarship was not the be all and end all of education at Ysgol Glasinfryn. We were introduced to a broader canvas than the 3Rs – to appreciate local history, music and literature. On the right as you entered the school there was a glass fronted cupboard, full of books, ranging from that great favourite *Llyfr Mawr y Plant* to E. Morgan Humphreys and Daniel Owen. The Headmaster himself was the author of several books for children which he tried out on us prior to publication. So we became literary critics at an early age. On the top shelf of the same cupboard there was a cane, but I never saw it used.

Glasinfryn School has now been closed and children from the area now attend the school at Llandygái.

Chapter 3

PENTIR VICARAGE

Pentir Vicarage is, in the jargon of Estate Agents, a house of character, built, so we are informed by the plaque, in 1890. It had several outbuildings and a paddock in addition to an extensive garden – relics of the days when the incumbent did a bit of farming on the side. The outbuildings made excellent play areas – here too we kept our "livestock". There were rabbits galore, which we entered for shows with moderate success.

We also kept a few hens, the gift of one of our layreaders, to help supplement the wartime rations. However, apart from a few eggs, we profited little from them as sources of food, because they became pets and members of the family, and we couldn't think of eating them. We also had a faithful mongrel dog, more spaniel than anything else, called Sandy who followed us wherever we went. To complete the menagerie, we had (for a few days) some racing pigeons. These were given to us by Auntie Sally's husband, Wilfred, who lived in Manchester and who was a great pigeon fancier. The instructions were to keep them in a shed for a week. This we did and eventually the great day came for the release. So we opened up the shed, out came the pigeons, they circled the shed a couple of times and that was the last we saw of them. A couple of hours later, Uncle Wilf was on the phone reporting that the pigeons were now back in Manchester!

Any dead animal or bird we found in the grounds was given a decent burial conducted with due solemnity. The dramatis personae were always the same – I, clad in black shirt, took the service. My cousin, Gwyneth, was the 'congregation' and Basil took the collection, if he hadn't already been kicked out for laughing before we reached that solemn point in the service.

Outside school hours we made our own entertainment. People often say that country children are fortunate in that they have the whole countryside as a vast play area, but this is misleading for as soon as they set foot in a field, more often than not would come a shout, "Clear off!" and we would hurry away. Much of our entertainment consisted of harmless pranks in which my brother Basil usually seemed to be the ringleader – knock doors, scrumping apples. Occasionally we would go up to Rhiwlas when there was a concert or Noson Lawen in the Institute, a corrugated iron structure which also served as a village hall. The thing to do then was to run around the building with a stick along the corrugations which made a thunderous noise inside.

I remember three shops there over the years. There was Siop Ann Hughes which she held in her front room in Rhyd-y-groes. A little further down the road in Queen's Terrace was Siop Jini Bwtchar, a rather straight laced lady who was a regular victim of Basil's pranks. I remember one occasion after a heavy fall of snow when he shovelled snow through her letter box and Jini chasing after him with a broom. The third shop I remember was the Post Office and General Store in the Square. It is now the Rainbow Café. Another of my little brother's victims was Llew the farm labourer at Bryn Howel, who once at Basil's teasing shouted in exasperation – "You little devil brought up on the Book of Common Prayer".

Using old pram wheels, we devised and constructed all kinds of Heath Robinson contraptions, such as trucks and rafts. We used to dam the river to form a pool. As these were war years every scrap of metal was needed for the war effort so our floats were rusty, leaking tin cans, which were more likely to sink our rafts than to keep them afloat. Another project we devised was a chip shop and we had visions of becoming great business tycoons, but alas the cooking fat, smuggled surreptitiously from our homes, caught fire on the opening night and that was the end of that.

One of the highlights of the year was the Sunday School trip to Rhyl and in order to increase our pocket money we would go up Moelyci, Pentir mountain to gather bilberries which we then took to Bangor to sell in the market where W. H. Smiths is now. There was also a Savings Club into which we put our pocket money in preparation for the trip. This was looked after by Richard Hughes, the caretaker at Pentir Church, and never was there a more reliable and faithful servant of the Church than he. But his English wasn't very good and he once introduced himself to some English visitors – "I'm the ring bellar here"! When he came out with some howler, Basil would say something like "Say that again Richard Hughes, I didn't hear you," just to hear him repeat the mistake. And while my father was away on Chaplaincy duty during the war there wasn't a night which went by that he didn't come round to the Vicarage to see that we were alright. He was a rare treasure.

Nansi Richards, (Telynores Maldwyn), lived for a time in Pentir and it was always a joy for us youngsters (unruly though we could be at times) to sit on the wall in front of her house, listening to her practising the triple harp, a very difficult art which few mastered – and we got it all for free.

Nothing is more indicative that one is growing old than finding items in a museum that one distinctly remembers in everyday use. In the world of farming we had threshing machines powered by a belt attached to a steam engine, the steamroller used in tarring roads, the horse-drawn plough and the pride the farm workers took in ploughing a straight furrow, the coming of the first tractor (Fordson). Then there was the excavator brought in to dig a cutting for the new bypass – the American Devil as it was called. These and more sophisticated machines are now two a penny on any building site but to us when we first saw them, they were great marvels.

When war broke out my father, who was on the reserved list, was called for military service immediately, but was turned down on health grounds, and it wasn't until later when the rules were relaxed that he was again called up to serve as an Army Chaplain, serving in Suffolk, Whitby (Yorkshire) and Tŷ-croes. We all as a family developed a great affection for Whitby which is a quaint little fishing village on the Yorkshire coast. When he could my father would arrange accommodation for us and we would then join him and enjoy an extended holiday together. But travel from Bangor to Whitby was difficult. A bomb on the track could play havoc with the timetable and when it was time to change trains, it was a case of each man for himself. More often than not it was standing room only on the incoming train. It was as we were engaged in such a dash that my brother Basil got separated from my mother and myself on York Station and was swallowed by the crowd. He was subsequently found by a porter and Basil asked him, "Have you seen my father, the Vicar of Pentir?" By some miracle the porter got him on to the right train.

The War years brought double summer time and 'daylight saving' which enabled agricultural work to be done at a late hour. I actually remember helping with the hay making at midnight! Then there was rationing and a points system to secure a fair share of food, clothing etc. for all. Rationing on some items continued for some time after the war was ended. Every one was urged to make the fullest use of their resources. 'Dig for Victory', 'Make do and mend' and 'Wage war on waste' became popular slogans.

From time to time the Ministry of Food issued recipes for all sorts of weird and wonderful things. Very often we would help my mother prepare what was known as War and Peace Pudding. She would mix dried fruit, spice, flour, suet, breadcrumbs, grated raw carrot, bicarbonate of soda and water, put the mixture into a bowl and steam it for at least two hours. It was barely palatable.

We regularly heard and saw German bombers passing overhead on their way to bomb Liverpool. From time to time a German raider would get into difficulty and would jetison its bombs at random in order to make a quick getaway. That is probably how a landmine came to be dropped on Maesgeirchen. There were blackout restrictions lest the least glimmer of light should help German bombers. Municipal shelters were built and in Pentir "Pharaoh" Jones, Bryn-glas, (a local farmer) took the initiative and built his own shelter. Identity cards were issued to everybody.

Those from large cities who were considered to be in particular danger were evacuated to the countryside, especially children and some from Liverpool came to Pentir. These were packed into trains and buses and on arrival at their destination they were subjected to pick your evacuee sessions, the more presentable being chosen and the grubby ones left behind. Understandably these children were often homesick but we did very little to alleviate their plight and the evacuees trickled back to their home towns. Our "evacuee" was our cousin Gwyneth whose home had been bombed in Holyhead.

It is interesting to note how much more sophisticated our communication systems are, compared with those days. Nowadays we are caught up in the heat of battle by means of video film and satellite. During the second World War, it was the radio that served as a lifeline. There were Churchill's morale boosting speeches. There was also Tommy Handley's 'ITMA' "It's that man again," (broadcast from Bangor), which became a feature of national life and more of a morale booster than some of the Government's propaganda efforts. A host of characters peopled the show and they and their catchphrases became part of the stuff of life – Mrs Mop the cleaner with her catchphrase "Can I do yer now Sir", Funf the bungling German spy, and Colonel Chinstrap with his "I don't mind if I do".

Eventually the momentous day came when the Germans surrendered in Europe (May 8th 1945 – Eiflyn's birth-day!) and the victory was celebrated by the ringing of the Church bells which had been silent through the war years, the lighting of bonfires, and the holding of street parties. But there was a price to be paid as Bob, one of the Storehouse boys, lost his life at Dunkirk, while Iorwerth, now the only surviving member of the family was awarded the Military Cross for distinguished service.

Chapter 4

FRIARS SCHOOL

So the years passed by and all too soon it became my turn to face up to the so called Scholarship, which would determine our scholastic and educational future. So in company with other candidates from the schools in the Bangor catchment area I duly turned up at Friars on the appointed day. This was the first time I had ever been there and I recall being particularly impressed by the size of everything as compared with what I was used to – there were more teachers there than pupils in Ysgol Glasinfryn and the whole of Ysgol Glasinfryn could have fitted nicely into a corner of the Friars Assembly Hall. However when the results came out, to my surprise, I found that I had been placed third in the (old) county of Caernarfon (first and second were Ken Evans and Elfed Humphries, both of Bangor). So I started on my first term at Friars, a building we shared for a time with the evacuated Liverpool Institute.

Friars School was founded by Geoffrey Glynne in 1557 "for the use of a Grammar School to be ever maintained in the said town of Bangor for the better education and bringing up of poor men's children." That was Friars school – the heir to a long and honourable history as a Grammar and Boarding School. It ceased to be a Boarding School about the time that I went there and there are horror stories of the quality of the catering during the latter years, including the lacing of Boss's beetroot with sherry by the Matron, Mrs Rees!

I got on reasonably well with most of the teachers except the Art master. Goodlad Dobson had his own way of remembering his new pupils' names. He had a theory that it would be easier for him to remember the names if the pupils were seated in alphabetical order so the process of sorting us out began. I missed out the E's but joined in with the R's. How was I to know that the surname of a little boy from Glasinfryn would not be used? When he came to doublecheck, my error was discovered much to his annoyance and he exploded in anger. Neither did my lack of artistic skill endear me to him as a star pupil. But come to think of it, L. S. Lowry didn't do too badly with his matchstick men!

During my time at Friars the Headmaster was Ivor Williams (Boss) who had been brought up in Hirael and was himself an old Friars boy. He was a graduate of Jesus College, Oxford and a notable Classics scholar who had served on the staff of Rossal School, Fleetwood before coming to Friars in 1934.

He was a great admirer of Winston Churchill whom he resembled physically. At the morning assembly, he would enquire who had heard the great man's address to the nation the previous evening and any poor wretch who hadn't would be held to public scorn and ridicule. He took a paternal interest in the fortune of old boys of the school serving in the armed forces, and we were regularly requested to bring fresh eggs to school which could be sent to those who were convalescing after war wounds.

E. W. Jones took the lower forms in Latin but the teaching of Latin in the higher forms was kept firmly in Boss' hands. He was an eccentric in many ways and had little time for anyone who didn't opt for Classics – as I chose Latin and Greek for 'Higher' I could do no wrong. He was also at times unpredictable. On a hot day he could stop in the middle of a lesson without warning and march half a dozen of us to Upper Bangor, together with his dog (Scott), buy a couple of ice creams and throw them to the dog, and then march us back to school again.

If Ivor noticed any children from Maes Tryfan (a council house estate nearby which was nicknamed Abyssinia) playing in the Friars grounds or in the plantation beside the annexe, he would send out some of the older boys to "capture" them and bring them before him to be told off in no uncertain terms. Such an action today would probably have landed him in court. "Catching Abyssinians" also became a game which helped the boarders to pass the weary evening hours.

Boss had little time for science, and music he regarded as a "cissy" subject, although the College Instrumental Trio were invited from time to time to demonstrate the finer points of music. Many old boys will remember Miss Constance Izzard and her pizzicato. But the whole thing was treated as a bit of a joke and teachers were stationed at strategic points of the Assembly Hall to keep order – and were probably as bored by the proceedings as we were.

A popular member of the staff was Harri Lloyd, the sportsmaster. We were fortunate to have him and his wife Ciss as our next door neighbours in Trefonwys, Bangor.

There was much coming and going among the members of the teaching staff as the younger ones were called up for military service and their places taken up by teachers called out of retirement. This proved to be a mixed bag, but among the oddities were some excellent teachers of long experience to whom we owe much. Among the odder retired teachers was a curious little man called Hewson, in many ways a pathetic figure and we used to play rings around him. A favourite prank was to put glue in his coffee mug, stir it well and stand back and await results. He must have had the constitution of an ox for he survived all this unscathed!

The Summer edition of the *Dominican* for 1948 shows that I took some part in the general life of the school. I was on the Editorial Committee of the Dominican, a member of the Senior Athletics team which took part in the Caernarfonshire Secondary Schools Championship and a poem I wrote is included. Not Shakespeare perhaps but a modest contribution. One notes that this is the only Welsh contribution in the whole magazine.

Chapter 5

MY VOCATION

As my time in Friars was coming to an end it was necessary to consider what my next step would be. Although there was no pressure put upon me, there was an unexpressed assumption that I would "go into the Church". Apart from my background there were other pointers in this direction too. One was the enthronement of Bishop J. C. Jones in Bangor Cathedral on January 27th 1949. Friars had been asked to send a representative of the school to the service and the Headmaster chose me. For a boy who had been brought up in a small country parish this was a splendid occasion – magnificent organ music, a packed church and a dignified if not mysterious ceremonial. Not that I ever had the slightest ambition to be a bishop, but this occasion seemed to me to show the Church in all its glory and I would be glad to be part of it. It was only later that I was to learn that the true glory of the Church belongs not to its pageantry and colour, (although these things have their place), but in its obedience to its Lord who is a servant King.

Then there was my father's sudden death in 1951 at the comparatively early age of 53. He was a much loved and devoted priest and by offering myself for Ordination I felt that I was carrying on the work which he had not been able to finish.

There were these little signs which seemed to me to point in the direction of Ordination – so I saw the Warden of Ordinands (John Charles), appeared before the Clerical Education Committee of the Diocese of Bangor and was duly received as an official candidate for Ordination.

Chapter 6

FROM PENTIR TO LLANFAIR-IS-GAER

After some 18 years in Pentir my father was offered the incumbency of Llanfair-is-gaer, to give the village its ecclesiastical title, (St Mary below the fort, i.e. Caernarfon Castle). An alternative name for the village is Y Felinheli (salt mill) – presumably because salt was extracted from the seawater there. It is interesting to note that salt production from seawater has been revived and is now served in top rank hotels and graces the tables of the great and the good. Yet another name is Port Dinorwic, i.e. the port from which the slate produced at the Dinorwic quarry was shipped all over the world. The Dinorwic quarry no longer operates and the port's only function today is as a marina.

There were three churches in the parish in our time – Llanfair Old Church, St Mary's Church and Port Church. Llanfair-is-gaer is a delightful old church on the shore of the Menai Straits. St Mary's was built nearer the centre of population and Port Church was built to minister to the spiritual needs of sailors, (now closed as a church and converted into a dwelling). There was also a private chapel on the Vaynol Estate, served, by arrangement, by the Vicar of the parish.

"A housegoing parson makes a churchgoing people", so says the old adage. My father was a conscientious parish priest and this was reflected in the congregation, and the Sunday evening service at St Mary's was a great joy and inspiration. We had just found our feet in our new parish and home, when the blow came in the sudden death of my father.

He had always been an early riser and so on this particular

morning he had got up as usual, lit the fire and put the kettle on to boil. When my mother got up a little later, she found him dead on the kitchen floor. Basil and I happened to be at home at the time and in a state of shock we called the doctor who was equally shocked, particularly as he (my father) had been in the surgery the previous evening with my brother who had a minor complaint, but had said nothing about being unwell himself.

We sent a message to Llanddeusant to inform my Auntie Mag who came over as soon as possible while my brother tried to contact Mr and Mrs Llew Rowlands (family friends who lived in Caernarfon) by phone. As there was a continuous engaged sound, Basil eventually cycled all the way to Caernarfon. I often think of that sad and lonely journey he made. It later transpired that our friends had taken their phone off the hook in order to have a lie in.

The immediate task was to arrange the funeral which we did with the assistance of the Bishop (J. C. Jones) and the Curate. But looking further ahead we had to arrange where we would live. At that time there was no Diocesan Housing Association which nowadays makes provision for clergy widows and thus takes away some of the pressures of a bereaved family. So the death of a cleric about fifty years ago not only meant the loss of a dwelling which went with the job but also the loss of the bread winner. After a short period of grace, the Parsonage had to be vacated. So the survivors had to find a roof over their heads as well as a means of support. I remember going with the Reverend O. H. Owen, who was my father's Assistant Curate to see Mr Emrys Williams of Gwyrfai Council to put our plight before him. Never could one have wished for a more understanding and sympathetic meeting and we were promised a house on the Wern Estate where the second phase of building was nearing completion. We have grateful memories of the kindness shown by the old Gwyrfai Council.

The next thing was to vacate the Vicarage and the simplest way to do this was to earmark what we wanted to take with us to Y Wern and to dispose of the remainder by public auction on the premises. At the appointed time the doors were opened and a crowd pressed forward into the porch, when suddenly the floor gave way and a number of people were pitched into the cellar and sustained various injuries. For some inexplicable reason the Auctioneer pressed on with the sale but as all attention was on the scene of the accident, the sale articles went for next to nothing, including a grand piano which was sold cheaply to a Chapel in Bangor. When O. H. Owen the curate went to see the Chapel officers to see if they would hand the piano back or offer a more realistic price, the answer was a firm "No". How greedy can one be and how different was the attitude of a secular body like Gwyrfai Council towards our predicament.

Then there was the matter of liability for the injured parties. It appears that what had happened was that someone in the past had laid tiles on a wooden floor which provided ideal conditions for dry rot to develop and with the weight of people pushing in, it gave way and pitched them into the cellar. When a few of the victims submitted claims for injuries the Church in Wales tried to foist responsibility on us, and it was a very harrowing situation coming on the heels of the bereavement. It was agreed by some that it was foolish to permit auction sales in Vicarages, but this was turned on its head by Canon Ben Jones, the former Vicar who still lived in the parish, who argued that it may be foolish to permit auction sales in Vicarages but not half as foolish as to lay tiles on a wooden floor! End of story and we heard no more about it, but in this episode as well as the piano incident the church didn't come out of it as a caring institution.

After this a new clause was added to the *Constitution of the Church in Wales* specifically forbidding sales by public auction in Vicarages and there it stands unto this day. At least we can claim to have been instrumental in getting an amendment to the Constitution – a notable achievement!

After settling into our new house, my mother resumed her career as a teacher, first as a supply and then in a permanent post at Aber-pwll, Port Dinorwic.

Chapter 7

UCNW BANGOR 1949-1952

The University College of North Wales, (as it was then known), was very different from the college we know today. For one thing it was much smaller, (about 900 students), and everyone knew everyone by sight if not by name. Today the student population is about 7,000 and the vast majority of those are non Welsh speakers.

For my first year I studied History (Prof. A. H. Dodd), Welsh (Prof., later Sir Thomas Parry), Greek (Prof. D. Wycherley) and Latin (Prof. M. L. Clark) – choosing Latin for my final year.

During my three years at UCNW, I stayed at the Church Hostel, (now the Anglican Chaplaincy), in Princes Road which was conveniently near the main College building. Although my home in Port Dinorwic was only a couple of miles down the road, my parents felt that I would miss out on an important element of College life and generously made provision for me to "live in".

There were a number of societies within the College which catered for all sorts of taste. There was the Welsh Society (Cymric) which offered a varied programme of distinguished speakers and Nosweithiau Llawen. There was an active Debating Society, and a number of religious societies which catered for all tastes – the Church Students Society (Anglican) based in the Church Hostel, the Student Christian Movement (SCM – ecumenical), the Inter Varsity Fellowship (IVF – fundamentalist).

The residents of the Church Hostel formed a family within a family and "freshers" were admitted to this select band in an initiation ceremony, the nature of which varied from year to year. The one devised for my year was to confiscate all the freshers' money, march us down to Bangor Station and here we were given a single ticket to Llanfair PG, put on the train and told to make our way back to Bangor and then we would be regarded as full members of the Hostel. All very well except that the train didn't stop at Llanfair PG but was non-stop to Holyhead! So we landed in Holyhead in the early hours of the morning without a penny between us and a useless ticket to Llanfair PG. There was nothing for it but to make a dash out of the station and start walking towards Bangor. To add to our predicament it started to pour with rain which made Bangor seem very far away. Fortunately for us, after we had gone a few miles, a merciful lorry driver stopped and gave us a lift to Bangor. I still have my single ticket to Llanfair PG as a momento of those happy days in the Hostel.

Another occasion for students' pranks was Menai Bridge Fair. The game here was to rope a couple of stalls together and to attach the other end of the rope to a passing bus. As the bus gathered speed it dragged the stalls with it to the understandable consternation of the stall holders. On the way back to Bangor we passed a petrol filling station with glass symbols of various petrol companies. These we would unscrew and then set up over the doorway of the Warden's flat.

Church Hostel students took a regular part in various college activities. They had a float in every Rag. I remember Alex Lewis as Queen Boadicea riding in a chariot drawn by the rest of us. I remember too Norman Hughes as a Flying Saucer pilot urging spectators to throw their gifts into the saucer. Both these became respectable Canons in the Church in Wales in later years.

Among the senior College staff, there were some notable figures in the academic world. There was Tom Parry, Head of the Welsh Department, a distinguished scholar with a heart of gold. When one of his students was taken ill through lack of adequate nourishment, Tom Parry invited him to join himself and his wife for Sunday lunch so that he got a nourishing meal once a week.

There was also Tom Richards who ruled the library with a rod of iron, and R. T. Jenkins an expert on Welsh history. Norman Denholme Young was a notable historian. Unfortunately we didn't see much of him as he spent most of his time at the summit of Snowdon because he claimed the whisky tasted better up there! Among the regular annual events was the Woolie Cup which was an excuse for a fight with the Normal College.

Women were strictly forbidden at the Hostel and the only time they were allowed in without let or hindrance was on the occasion of the annual Christmas Party. For this all the men were required to invite a girl – failure to do so would incur a heavy fine and a girl would be found for you. The ploy was to stand outside the chapel after the Sunday morning service, select a girl of one's choice and that would be that. As I had no regular girl friend I used the selection process and was delighted when a pretty blonde student teacher accepted my invitation. Apart from the occasional letter and cards, we lost touch for a long time and the next time I saw her was to swear her in as a Church Warden – that was one of my more interesting Archdeacon's visitations thirty years later.

Despite fooling around and enjoying myself, I also worked hard and graduated in 1952 with 1st Class Honours in Latin. It is sad to reflect that Latin is no longer taught at Bangor and that one must go to Durham to study Latin at University level.

Chapter 8

OXFORD 1952-1954

As I would have been too young to be ordained immediately after completion of my course at Bangor, John Charles who was then Warden of Ordinands for Bangor and St Asaph as well as Warden of the Church Hostel advised me to use the "spare" year at Oxford reading Theology. The Oxford College with the strongest Welsh connection is Jesus, but John Charles encouraged me to apply to Keble which was his old College

Keble is one of the younger colleges, founded in 1870, designed by William Butterfield in memory of John Keble, one of the leaders of the Oxford Movement – a movement within the Church of England which aimed at restoring the High Church ideals of the 17th century. So I applied to Keble and was duly accepted.

Much of college life revolved around the dining hall and chapel and one was expected to attend both. An attendance list recorded one's presence or otherwise in chapel. One of the notable features of the chapel was that it contains Holman Hunt's famous painting 'The Light of the World'. There is another version of this painted some 40 years after the Keble one in St Paul's Cathedral.

The Warden of Keble during my time there was Harry Carpenter, later Bishop of Oxford, who was married to Urith the daughter of G. M. Trevelyan, the historian. They had a son Humphrey, whom I remember as a rather naughty little boy who derived great pleasure in throwing stones at students on their way to chapel! He is now a distinguished historian.

Most of the teaching was by way of the tutorial system. The

lecture timetable was formidable and it would have been impossible to have attended them all. Under the guidance of one's tutor one would make a selection of what would be most useful for the essay the tutor had set for the week, while on the hour there were fleets of cycles going from one lecture to another. My tutor at Keble was the College Chaplain, the Rev. G. C. Stead who was a keen train spotter.

There were also visiting lecturers, many of them distinguished speakers and authorities in their particular field. So I attended some lectures by C. S. Lewis and by Bishop A. M. Ramsey, later to become Archbishop of Canterbury. Among the tutors were some genuine eccentrics. It is said of one that when his pupil entered the tutor's room he could see no-one, but he eventually found his tutor sitting under a table and from there the tutorial was conducted!

But I didn't enjoy my time at Oxford and missed Bangor terribly – perhaps not all Oxford's fault but the general atmosphere was not for me. What saved my sanity was the Welsh Society, the famous Cymdeithas Dafydd ap Gwilym, 'Y Dafydd', whose patron was Idris Foster, a native of Bethesda and Professor of Celtic at Jesus. I was very proud to have been elected Treasurer of the Society,

There were personal factors which had also contributed to my unhappiness. I was concerned for my recently widowed mother. My brother Basil after completing his training on HMS Conway was away at sea and Oxford seemed very far from Port Dinorwic. There was also probably delayed shock at my father's sudden death and all the upheaval and anxiety of finding a home and moving. As I had already graduated at the University of Wales I was allowed to take my Oxford Degree in two rather than three years.

All this inevitable pressure of work took its toll on my physical health and when I returned home at the end of my time in Oxford, the family had the shock of their lives when this emaciated figure arrived on their doorstep. My mother later told me that she had barely recognised me, so it was all hands on deck to build me up again. As my mother was out teaching all day and could ill afford to miss school, Auntie Mag and Uncle Owie took me to Valley where they had moved to following Uncle Owie's retirement as Headmaster of Llanddeusant school. The treatment was, a lie in every morning and a cup of raw egg beaten with sherry. After lunch a walk with Uncle Owie, then a lazy and relaxing evening playing games, (Scrabble or Monopoly). Three weeks of this put me on my feet again and despite the near breakdown, I obtained a 2nd in Theology and was awarded the Wills Theological Prize, but it was not an experience I would wish to repeat.

Chapter 9

LLANDAFF – STUDENT 1954-1955

After completing my degree at Oxford in 1954, my next move was to a Theological College and the one chosen for me was St Michael's College, Llandaff.

Theological Colleges as we have come to know them are a product of the nineteenth century. They are not owned by the Church but are private foundations designed to provide vocational training as opposed to a general education. Such was St Michael's College which was founded in Aberdare in 1892, but moved to Llandaff in 1907.

During a bombing raid on Cardiff in the evening of January 2nd 1941, what is believed to have been a land mine struck the south west corner of the Quadrangle, inflicting heavy damage to all parts of the building. The Cathedral was also extensively damaged in the same raid. Fortunately there was no one in residence otherwise there would have been a heavy loss of life, but the college was rendered homeless. Temporary accommodation was found first in St David's and then at Llys Esgob, now the Cathedral School, into which about twenty students were packed living two or three to a room. This fostered an atmosphere of friendship and fellowship which I hadn't experienced at Oxford.

The basic course was the G.O.E. – General Ordination Examination, irreverently referred to as God's Own Examination. This involved a study of the Old Testament, New Testament, Church History, Liturgy, Doctrine and Ethics. There were also lectures in various aspects of Pastoralia. Our daily timetable was as follows:

7.00	Prime
7.15	Holy Communion
7.50	Matins
8.15	Breakfast
9.30-10.00	Quiet time for private devotion
10.00- 1.00	Study and Lectures
1.00	Sext
1.15	Luncheon
4.30	Tea
5.00	Study
6.30	Evensong
7.00	Dinner
8.00	Study
9.30	Compline

The College Visitor was John Morgan, Archbishop of Wales and Bishop of Llandaff. He was seen by many as a bit of a martinet, although I found him to be kindly and approachable. He had a thing about clergy being properly dressed and this included wearing a hat, and woe betide anyone seen without one. There was a story, probably apocryphal, of him seeing a man with a clerical collar but no hat in one of the Cardiff streets. John stopped his car in the middle of the traffic and tore a strip off him only to find too late that he wasn't an Anglican cleric but a nonconformist minister.

As I said, in my dealings with him, few as they were, I found him helpful and considerate. I remember one occasion which reflected this. As part of our pastoral training we were required to take part in a parish placement, i.e. to work in a parish for a short period to get a taste of parish life. I was assigned to take part in a parish mission, led by Father Silyn SSF. At the opening service of the mission the Archbishop was to commission the mission team, and he undertook to give me a lift from Llandaff to Aberdare for the commissioning service. It was a bitterly cold night and the Archbishop, (by then a very frail and sick man), noticing my chattering teeth, took off his cloak and wrapped it round me. So much for the martinet.

We had had some instruction in the art of preaching in Theological College and taken part in sermon classes when we had preached before our fellow students and received their criticisms. We had also gone out with a member of staff to preach at 'a proper service' in a country church. But this also had its limitations – one was distracted by the staff member making notes on his writing pad. Was he making a note of some new heresy that had been uttered or some brilliant exposition that had just been made? Of course, it was, and is, possible to buy books of sermons but here it is important to read through these sermons carefully before hand, and make these your own – it is rather disastrous for a young curate to start his sermon "When I was bishop of Lebombo"! I overheard the Vicar's wife comment to one of the parishoners after the service – "at least it was his own sermon", an example of being damned with faint praise.

One of the interesting things about Church life in the Diocese of Llandaff was that you could experience the vast variety of Churchmanship within the Anglican Communion and most of the students at St Michael's College took the opportunity of sampling what was on offer in the various churches. One such church was Dewi Sant, the only Welsh language Church in Cardiff. The original church in Howard Gardens was severely damaged in a wartime bombing raid and found a new home in the nearby St Andrews. This was the Dewi Sant I knew when I was in Llandaff.

The fame of Eglwys Dewi Sant had spread far beyond the confines of Cardiff thanks to the pastoral and preaching gift of the Vicar, Canon Reginald Rosser. He was much in demand as a harvest preacher and any parish that managed to secure his services counted itself most blessed.

I remember one vivid sermon of his on prayer. He depicted God in a great big office surrounded by telephones and gadgets galore, (there were no computers in those days), "Who's there? Reginald Rosser wants a word with God. Put him through." And he had a marvellous series of sermons on the Psalms which started when I first went to Dewi Sant and was still going strong ten years later.

Then while Reginald Rosser performed his prophetic ministry in the pulpit, his wife Emily was at the Church door exercising her ministry of welcome, checking up on who was there and who wasn't. We talk these days of team ministry. They had it in Reginald and Emily Rosser long ago.

Chapter 10

GLANADDA – CURATE 1955-1957

In the happy atmosphere of St Michael's, time flew by and it soon became necessary to decide on the parish I would serve in on my Ordination. Bishop J. C. Jones' original proposal was that I should go to Machynlleth, but my father's untimely death changed all that as the Bishop felt it would take me too far from my mother, so Glanadda was substituted for Machynlleth, and this proved to be a happy choice for me. So I was ordained deacon in St Mary's Church, Llanfair-is-gaer on Trinity Sunday 1955 along with another Ordinand, Raymond Byles who was Curate of the parish. I was to serve in the parish of Glanadda, Bangor.

The completion of the main line Railway system, from London to Holyhead saw the development of Bangor as a railway town, especially the West end of the City. Until fairly recently the station and goods yard was a hive of activity with trains coming and going not only on the main lines but also on the branch lines. There was the clank of waggons as trucks were sent careering down the goods yard line to form a goods train, and more recently, diesel units were shunted and coupled together. The rail yard was a place of fun and friendly banter, and an unguarded word or comment could land one with a nickname for life, for example Bobi Joy, Will Noble. At that time about 150 men were employed in the station and the platform staff were always smartly dressed in their uniforms.

The station formed a community within the larger community of Bangor and it was to meet the needs of this expanding area that the parish of Glanadda was formed out of the old parish of Bangor to become a parish in its own right.

The Branch lines slowly disappeared thanks to Dr Beeching, as Caernarfon, Llangefni, Gaerwen, Amlwch, Bethesda stations and the like were closed, and the main line station was left in splendid isolation. The sounds and smells of the old steam years will not be easily forgotten. Nor will the splendid workers that went with them.

St David's church was built in 1888 as a memorial to Dean H. T. Edwards. Also incorporated in the new parish was the area known as Penrhosgarnedd which already had a church, which was a corrugated iron structure, ten years before St David's was built. This was replaced by a brick building during my time as curate there. All the bricks were donated by Sir Michael Duff. This was St Peter's Church which is still remembered with affection by the older members of the community.

My first problem was to find accommodation, for in those days there was no automatic provision for housing curates – you found your own, and for this I was assigned a yearly stipend of £330 per annum. After some searching, (much of the accommodation in Bangor was snapped up by students), I eventually found a place with Mr and Mrs Tom Parry, 16 Penrhos Road and they looked after me in kindly and homely fashion.

A car was useful if not essential and motor expenses had to be paid out of the annual salary. All fees belong by right to the incumbent, although Gilbert, if he was in a generous mood would pass the minister's fee on to me. This came in the form of a brown 10 shilling note equivalent to what today is 50 pence. If the pair getting married wanted any extras, e.g. red carpet, bells, choir, there was an additional payment to the basic marriage fee.

On my first day I was taken by my Vicar (Evan Gilbert Wright) to the Church Hall at St David's, (a kind of crypt under the Church), and told to get on with building a stage – a Heath Robinson contraption of wooden planks resting on brick pillars – ready for some concert which the Sunday School was putting on. And off he went, leaving me to it.

I felt very lonely and depressed, asking myself the question – "Is this what I have been ordained for?" But there was method in the madness for it reminded me at the outset that ministry involves getting one's hands dirty.

Although a native of South Wales, Gilbert spent his ministry in this diocese, in Llangefni, Gaerwen and Glanadda. He was a historian and had graduated in Liverpool with a thesis on Bishop Humphrey Humphreys. For many years he was Secretary of the Anglesey Antiquarian Society, and from time to time he would land a bundle of letters giving notice of some meeting or other, and my task was to address all the envelopes.

He was a stickler for punctuality and all meetings started bang on time. If not, out would come a surly "You're late man!" Similarly if he had arranged a baptism for a certain time and the baptismal party hadn't arrived by the appointed hour, he would storm home. Sometimes he would meet the baptismal party only a few yards from the church. "Try again next Sunday," he would say and continue on his way. And I don't think he would have much to say for the present day emphasis on shared ministry. Any argumentative member of the P.C.C. would be shot down with: "Who is Vicar here; you or me?" And that would be the end of that. I saw him once called to the hospital and being told by a nurse, "The doctor is on the ward." And Gilbert responded "His time is no more important than mine," and stormed into the ward.

For the incumbent, the arrival of a new curate was a mixed blessing. It meant an extra pair of hands, but it also meant a new pair of hands to be trained in the realities of parish life and from that point of view, in many ways it would have been easier to have done the task oneself! The arrival of a new curate was also good news for any females aged between eight and eighty who had a great appetite for anything wearing a clerical collar. In Glanadda there was a plentiful supply of young nurses attached to the local hospital as well as the young ladies resident in the parish. All these had to be dealt with, with tact and discretion, and in some instances I, like many a young curate, had to tread with caution.

Gilbert was also a great believer in visiting and curates were expected to be likewise. As usually happened in most parishes the curate was entrusted with the care of the youth club – Glanadda was no exception. We had a small but very active youth group who played a central part in the life of the parish, organising evening mystery trips and other social activities. They were also very regular in attendance at the church services.

One very faithful member was Pam Lane, the churchwarden's daughter who had a congenital heart defect and who went about in an old fashioned invalid chair. We would never have thought of going anywhere without Pam and the concern and love of those youngsters gave Pam a full and meaningful life.

Inevitably there were many things which I would be doing for the first time during my first curacy. One of these was the weekly sermon which seemed to take a disproportionate amount of time to prepare.

The building of the new St Peter's Church in Penrhosgarnedd made a heavy financial demand on the parish and there was a constant round of fêtes, rummage sales and other money raising events. One major event was a Fête at Vaynol Park which was arranged with military precision by Major Buckland. Instructions would be sent out in military style such as – " The men shall assemble at eighteen hundred hours equipped with hammers, saws and other tools".

I soon found out that when there was a Rummage Sale, it was the curate's job to run a collecting service of goods.These efforts were so well established that there was never a need for any committee to organise them. They just happened!

The 'customers' were kept out of the Church Hall until the official starting time and as the crowd grew larger, the banging on the door and the language grew fruitier and fruitier. Indeed they could have rivalled any Sergeant Major. It was also my job to get rid of the unsold goods which were by ancient custom "sold en bloc" to an old girl who was a regular attender at these functions. To the Vicar's great displeasure one over-enthusiastic 'sales girl' managed to sell his hat!

But it wasn't all money raising. The general life of the parish had to go on, the sick had to be visited, the dead buried and services maintained.

When I first went to the parish, Penrhosgarnedd was a self contained village on the outskirts of Bangor with a distinctive character of its own. It had its village school (Vaynol) and a leading figure in the community was the Headmaster (William Pritchard) an excellent churchman, but a bit sombre, and Gilbert used to play on this unmercifully. I remember him on one occasion taking me to see William Pritchard who was upstairs in bed with flu. As we went upstairs, Gilbert turned to Mrs Pritchard and said in a loud stage whisper: "Difficult stairs to bring a coffin down!" William Pritchard made an instant recovery.

One of the characters at Penrhos was John Williams (John Bung). John was a bit simple yet in his own way he was all there. We had a great deal of fun with John but in no way would anyone treat him with ridicule. He was the bellringer at St Peter's and he would come out with some perceptive observations. Mrs Annie Hughes farmed Maes Mawr with her husband Robert, (a housing estate has now taken over the farmland). Mrs Hughes was a regular worshipper at St Peter's but usually arrived late. But on one occasion she arrived early. John noticed this and went up to her with a comment, "Well Mrs Hughes, nice to see you come early for a change!"

Getting books ready for the service, he would ask, "Is it Litany or Matinee this morning"! He couldn't tell the time so he would come to the Vestry and ask if it was time to ring the bell. I replied "You'd better wait a bit John". A couple of minutes later he would come to ask the same question and got the same answer. This went on three or four times and at last John demanded, "Why can't I ring the bell now?" and I replied "Well you see, the chapel service has started and we don't want to disturb them". To which John responded, "To hell with the chapel. Church comes first", and hauled the bell furiously until the old tin Church shook.

We used to go carol singing around the parish in aid of the Children's Society. John always came with us and his job was to go to houses with the collecting tin. When we were singing outside the house of one woman who made herself out to be somebody rather posh, John suddenly shouted, "Alright boys, stop singing. She only put 2 pence in the box." The lady retired in shame and confusion!

My first interview to arrange a wedding was a bit of a disaster. I was reading quietly in my digs one evening, (the theological college had stressed the importance of keeping up our reading), when the doorbell rang and on the doorstep stood a young couple whom I had never seen before. I invited them to come in and sit down and they started on their story. The girl soon burst into tears while the young man became quite aggressive. Thrusting his fist under my nose he demanded, "She *must* marry me and you must make her marry me." By now I felt that the situation was running out of my control and the best thing was to play for time. So I told them to come and see me on such and such a day and time, and by then I would have got the necessary papers.

So the following day I went to see John Richards, Vicar of St James and later Bishop of St David's and asked him what I should do. "Don't worry, my boy," he said, "it happens to all of us. I found myself in a similar situation when my Vicar was away on holiday. All I could think of doing was to send him a telegram, 'Churchwarden eloped with organist, donkey dead, return at once'."

From then on I experienced several amusing events in connection with weddings. There was the old boy who when I asked him if they wanted banns or licence, replied "Thank you Vicar, but we want a quiet wedding. We don't want a band."

I soon found out that being curate of Glanadda involved one in many non-ecclesiastical activities. Gilbert would suddenly decide to go pheasant shooting and we would take up our station at the foot of the Vaynol wall with the object of taking a pot shot at Sir Michael Duff's pheasants as they flew over the wall. Alas I was in far greater danger than the pheasants. I asked him what I was expected to do if a pheasant was shot and he replied, "Put it into your bag and run like hell!"

Then fishing would capture his fancy and we would make our way to the River Ogwen and more often than not end up in an icy pool to the amusement of some spectators on the bank who were watching the show

The Vicarage family were very fond of animals especially horses. These were kept at Pentraeth where the Vicar had a small field. From time to time it was necessary to exercise the horses by giving them a canter on the beach – Red Wharf Bay, which was ideal for the purpose. They owned the horses and as they were one rider short on this particular occasion, I was persuaded against my better judgement to ride the third horse while the Vicar's wife and daughter rode the other two. So we made our way to the beach and the two women went on ahead while my horse ambled along at a gentle pace. Suddenly he seemed to sense that he was being left behind and he shot forward to catch up with them. I grabbed hold of the only secure thing which was the rear of the saddle and clinging on for dear life I proceeded at considerable speed back to front!

One of my tasks when the Vicarage family was on holiday, was to look after the Vicarage dog – a mixture of varieties and called Heinz for obvious reasons. On one occasion when I was taking him out for a walk I was attacked by another dog. I was badly bitten on my leg and I carry the scars to this day.

Chapter 11

LLANDAFF – STAFF 1957-1966

So there I was, happily settled as Curate of Glanadda with Penrhosgarnedd when out of the blue came a letter from the Warden of St Michael's College, Llandaff, (John Charles), inviting me to join the teaching staff of the College. I hesitated long over this for several reasons: I was perfectly happy where I was and the thought of an academic career had never crossed my mind. Had I what it takes for such a post? Further, I was only a couple of years older than many of the students and younger than several of them, and could I cope with that? Again all my connections were with North Wales and I knew nothing of South Wales and didn't particularly want to either. The more I pondered the more confused I became so I took the problem to the Bishop, then G. O. Williams, which I would have been bound to do anyway and his advice was – "I'm not telling you to go, but if I were you I would go." So I packed my bags in 1957 and headed south, little thinking that Glanadda would see me again in a few years time. In the meantime, John Charles, the Warden who appointed me, had left St. Michael's on his appointment as Dean of St Asaph, and it was his successor, O. G. Rees who inherited me. My first year as a Lecturer was heavy going as it involved preparing lectures from scratch and keeping a few pages ahead of the class.

An important development during my time there was the link established with the University School of Theology and men at St Michael's were prepared not only for the General Ordination Examination but also for the University of Wales Diploma in

Theology and B.D., and the staff of St Michael's became accredited teachers in the School of Theology. Our partners in this were the members of the South Wales Baptist College who formed the other half of the School of Theology. This link with the University was significant for it brought St Michael's out of its splendid isolation, but it also necessitated an adjustment in the dates of St Michael's terms to bring them into line with the University terms. One consequence of this was the dropping of the fourth term to correspond with the University's pattern of residence. This affected in particular our traditional observance of Holy Week and Easter.

For over a century the idea of a Theological College was of a semi-monastic community, people living under one roof worshipping, and praying and studying together. But the 1960's saw a change of emphasis as the regime became more liberalised. No longer were students compelled to study in the evenings, but were free to go to the theatre or cinema while they were expected, but not compelled, to attend the services in the College Chapel. Another outward and visible sign of the new relaxed discipline was the growing provision of married quarters. Wives and girl friends were welcome guests at meals. The Cook's College, or The College of Domestic Arts as it was officially called, up the road provided a ready source of the latter, and the Sunday morning Eucharist became virtually a Family Communion.

This period saw the completion of the new Chapel, designed by George Pace, the Llandaff Cathedral Architect. It was consecrated on the 2 February 1959 by Glyn Simon, Bishop of Llandaff and the preacher was the Warden of Keble College, Oxford, Eric Abbott.

When I joined the staff of St Michael's I was licensed by the Bishop of Llandaff to officiate generally in the Diocese. This gave me an opportunity to get to know the Diocese reasonably well and also to experience the great variety of churchmanship to be found in the Diocese which ranged from "bells and smells" on the one hand and celebrating Eucharists at the North end of the Lord's table on the other.

From time to time a member of the altar party would come into the Sanctuary and hold up in front of me some ecclesiastical garment or article such as a thurible. Not being very clear what I was supposed to do with them, I devised for myself a rule of thumb: If you can wear it, wear it; if you can shake it, shake it. If you can't wear it or shake it, kiss it. If nothing else, such experience reminded one of the rich variety of the church.

If the Church of Dewi Sant represents one facet of the ecclesiastical spectrum, St Mary's Cardiff Docks, St German's and St Stephen's represent the opposite extreme. Although its churchmanship is not mine I have a soft spot for St Stephen's for it was there that I preached my first three hour devotion. My main worry was not the preparation of the service but would I physically be up to a long service? So I went to the pulpit armed with nutritious groceries – chocolates, glucose and fruit, until it looked more like a grocer's shop than a church pulpit. However it did the trick and I survived.

The teaching staff remained virtually unchanged throughout my time at St Michael's. The Warden, Geoff Rees taught Church History. The Sub-warden, H. Lewis Clarke taught New Testament. He later became Archdeacon of Llandaff. Also for a period there was John Poole Hughes (later Bishop of Llandaff), the Chaplain J. C. Mears (later Bishop of Bangor) taught Doctrine, a kind and good friend, and there was myself as Librarian, teaching Old Testament and anything else which the Warden found needed doing!

There was considerable rivalry between the kitchen staff led by the cook, Miss Pugh, (later Mrs Spillman) and the Housekeeping staff led by Mrs Ella Hunter. The old hands amongst the students recognised the danger signs when a storm was about to break, and took evasive action, but for those caught in the eye of the storm, it was quite an experience.

But there were more problems ahead. Gilbert Wright, my first Vicar was appointed as Archdeacon of Bangor and moved to the small parish of Abergwyngregyn, and I was appointed to take his place at Glanadda. This was for me a crucial decision for it meant making a choice between academic life and a pastoral ministry. So after ten years in St Michael's, I packed up my lecture notes and took my leave of the College.

Nain Holyhead.

Nain Llanddona.

Taid Holyhead.

Taid Llanddona.

Dad.

Mam.

My parents' wedding.

Pentir Vicarage.

My parents and myself at Pentir.

With Sandy the family pet.

When I was
2 years old.

With Jennie the maid at
Pentir.

Basil as a baby.

Basil when he was 5 years old.

With Gwyneth and Basil in the
garden at Pentir.

With my cousin Gwyneth.

Glasinfryn School, 1940.

Row 1: Keith Heyward, Glyn Johns, Neville Bowen, Joe Evans, Gwilym Hughes, Ken Williams, Basil Roberts, Owie Williams.
Row 2: Eric Parry, Vernon Moore, Menna Roberts, Gracie Williams, Eurwen Jones, Rowena Owen, Doris Williams, ?, Beti Roberts, Mary Jones, Gerald Roberts.
Rhes 3: Eirwen Hughes, Dilys Jones, Elsa Moore, Nancy Buckley, Glenys Davies, Nellie Hughes.
Row 4: Miss Hughes, Elwyn Roberts, Dafydd Roberts, Nancy Hughes, Dilys Rowlands, Hilda Hughes, Joan Bowen, John Dennis Williams, Robert Williams, Ron Moore, Hugh Vaughan Roberts, the Headmaster.

The Curate O. H. Owen, with Basil and myself on the Sunday School trip to Rhyl.

My parents at Felinheli Vicarage.

Some of the pupils and staff at Friars, Bangor, 1946.

Back row: W. J. Fedrick, D. H. Owen, R. Muir, T. Vaughan Edwards, J. D. Williams, Elwyn, Arwyn Owen, Doug Thomas, P. Thomas, Ken Evans, R. C. Wilson, R. H. Jones, John M. Jones, John L. Evans.

Staff: Park Jones, Alan Nicholas, A. R. Davies, Edmund Humphreys, J. Lowe, E. R. Williams, J. R. Griffiths, Miss Potter, Ivor Williams (Headmaster), J. R. Fielding, Coulter, E. W. Jones, Ned Darke, Ward.

My 18th Birthday.

Below left:
Basil aboard ship.

Below: Gwyneth and myself in Chester.

Students of the Church Hostel, Bangor, 1950.

David James, Gwyn Francis, ?, Maurice Osborne, ?, Leslie Edwards, George Jones, Elwyn Jones, John Birkenshaw, ?. George Sage, George de Burgh Thomas, Norman Hughes, Parch. Charles, Alex Lewis, L. P. Jones. Gerald Miles Davies, Gwilym Jones, Margaret, Wyn Jones, Elwyn, Tom Roberts.

College Rag Procession, 1950.

A student at Oxford, 1953.

Graduation Day in Bangor, 1952.

'Cymdeithas Dafydd ap Gwilym', Oxford, 1953.
?, Tom Closs, Tom Bowen, Richard Jones, ... Evans.
Ellis Evans, ?, ?, Gwyn Jones, David Evans, Ednyfed Hudson Davies, John Tudor.
Brynley Jones, ?, Professor Idris Foster, Brychan Hughes, Elwyn.

Graduation Day at Oxford, 1954.

Recuperating in Llanddeusant,
summer 1954.

My 21st Birthday.

Mam, Anti Mag, myself and Uncle Owie at Cable Bay.

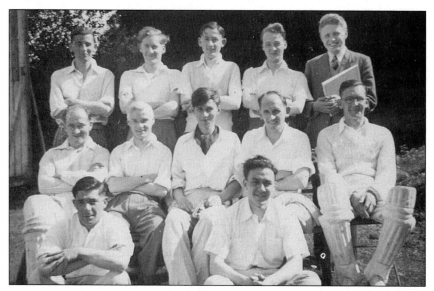

St. Michael's College, Llandaff – Cricket team, 1955.

The Chapel of St Michael's College, Llandaff
designed by George G. Pace, the Cathedral Architect.

Above:
The day of my Ordination, 1955.

Above right:
With Bishop J. C. Jones when he laid the foundation stone of St Peter's Church, Penrhosgarnedd.

Right:
Gilbert Wright, William Pritchard and myself in Penrhosgarnedd.

Bishop G. O. Williams prior to the opening service at St Peter's Church Penrhosgarnedd, 1956.
Sir Michael Duff, Gilbert Wright, Elwyn, Bishop Gwilym, Meurig Foulkes, Bill Lane, Colonel Cartrer, Victor Edwards, P. M. Padmore.

St Michael's College Llandaff – Soccer team, 1959.
L. Rogers, S. Wilcox, M. Boit, Lionel, R. Rowlands, Cledan Mears.
Elwyn Roberts, S. Gilbert, F. Mudge, O. G. Rees, Glyn Jones, D. Humphreys,
Eurwyn Thomas.

St Michael's College Llandaff – Soccer team, 1965.

Staff and Students at St Michael's College, Llandaff, 1957/58.

Thomas Pierce, David John, Ernest Brown, Brian Evason, R. Bullivant, F. W. Biddlecombe, L. P. Ford, H. G. Roberts, D. A. Bates, W. J. Twidell, David Williams.

W. J. Loyns, Arthur Morgan, Geoffrey Bainbridge Evans, Paul Wilkinson, Kerry Goulstone, Alfred Hawkins, Neville Thomas, Elwyn John, J. E. Jones.

Glyn Martin, Alwyn R. Jones, Robert Glyn Owen, Graham Davies, L. T. G. Evans, Dudley White, David Jones, John Thomas, Brian Morris, John Taylor, Edward Hunt, G. Amos, Malcolm Beynon, Erwyd Edwards, Martin Bowen, O. G. Rees, J. Poole Hughes, Elwyn Roberts, Derek Walker, Richard Hughes, Robert Williams.

Staff and Students at St Michael's College, Llandaff, 1959/60.

Brian Williams, Gwyn Ll. Jones, Brian Dodsworth, Sidney Wilcox, D. G. Prosser, Irfon Parry, Brian Jones, David Jenkins,
Geoffrey Thomas, Gareth Lewis, Eurwyn Thomas, Brian Jones, Llew Roberts, Eric Wastell, R. Hanson.
R. Rowlands, Eddie Smart, R. J. E. W. Rees, Mervyn Boit, L. Ford, L. Webber, A. Hughes, John Gilpin, G. Jones, Basil Harris,
B. Snaith, Syd Gilbert.
Gerald Lovitt, Philip Brian Jones, Trefor Richardson, Cledan Mears, Lewis Clarke, O. G. Rees, Elwyn Roberts, William Spillman,
Fred Mudge, D. Humphries, Peter Ungoed Thomas.
Geoff Swindley, W. Twidell, Neville Jones, James McDonald, Brian Hall, Tom Stilling, James Coutts, R. H. Woodall.

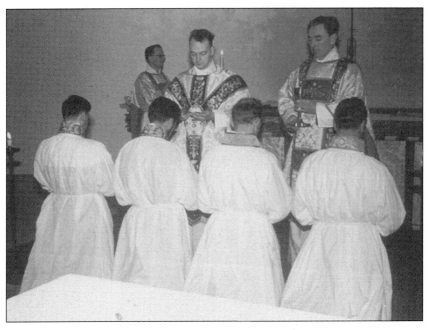

First Evensong of a Saint's Day at St Michael's College Chapel, Llandaff.

A baptism at
St David's Church,
Glanadda.

Our Wedding Day at Holy Trinity Church, Llandudno, October 16, 1971.

The ushers at our wedding: John, Stephen, Ifan.

Wedding Group.
Bishop Gwilym, my Mother, Judith, Dr Elwyn, Myself, Eiflyn, Olwen, Eiflyn's Grandmother, Richard, Eiflyn's Mother. Berwyn, Bethan.

Mid-service Training Course at St George's House, Windsor, 1974.

Llinos, born on July 12, 1976.

Llinos' Christening, September 1976.

Sioned, born on April 2, 1982.

Below:
Sioned's Christening, July 1982.

With the girls, 1983.

Cleaning St Tudno's Church for the summer.
Bill and Iona Harris, Geraldine Meikle, myself and the girls.

A group of young wives from the parish who sang regularly
at St Tudno's Church.
Denise Templeton, Sue Turner, Susan Williams, Sandra Davies, Barbara Jones,
Jill Paddock, Eiflyn.

Conducting a service at St Tudno's Church.

With Archbishop Gwilym in Holy Trinity Church.

The Choir of St George's Church, Llandudno, 1981.
Blodwen Williams, Glyn Goodier, Elwyn Parry, John Harvey, R. Evans Thomas,
Geoff Templeton, Steven Griffith, Bill Harris, Christine Jones.
Effie Rowlands, Marie Swaine, Daniel Davies, Eileen Joyce, Madge Owen,
Stephanie Littlewood.

The Choir of Holy Trinity Church, Llandudno, 1979.

Ken Docksey, Margaret Cross, Harold Barton, Fred Cross, Ray Stythe Jones, Sam Joule, Clive Roberts, John Clutton, Stan Riley, Fred Allman, Awena Hughes.

John Evans, Lena Williams, Jean Jones, Mrs. Penry Hughes, Phyllis Hart, Geraldine Meikle, Marjorie Birchall, Gaynor Stythe Jones, Bill Lord.

Peter Brookes, June Griffith, Gwilym Berw Hughes, Elwyn, R. Evans Thomas, Gareth Hughes. Einir Hughes, Gillian Brookes, Marc Hughes, Melvyn Kelly.

Archbishop G. O. Williams and the Bangor Cathedral Chapter, 1978.
Tommy Morris, Norman Hughes, Elwyn, Alwyn Rice Jones, Michael Preece, Alun Jones, Hywyn Jones, John Vevar, W. R. Hughes, R. D. Roberts.
Meurig Foulkes, Archdeacon Arfon Evans, Deon Ifor Rees, Archbishop Gwilym O. Williams, R. Dwyfor Jones, Archdeacon T. Bayley Hughes, Glyndwr Williams.

Shrove Tuesday in the parish of Criccieth, 1984.
Gwen Herbert, Beti Smith, Agnes Ellis, Olive Mayne, Muriel Mayne, Mattie Mckie,
Marguerite Jones preparing the pancake batter in the Rectory.

Harvest Supper at Criccieth, October 1985.

Kate's
Wedding
in
London,
1984.

Celebrating my mother's 80th birthday.

Cledan and myself walking up Snowdon.

Bishop Cledan and the Bangor Cathedral Chapter, 1988.
Andrew Jones, William Jones, Richard Jones, Alex Lewis, Hywyn Jones, Geraint Vaughan Jones, Robert Williams,
Elwyn Roberts, Len Arridge.
John F. W. Jones, Meurig Foulkes, Archdeacon Elwyn, Deon Ivor Rees, Esgob Cledam, Trevor Evans, Archdeacon Barry, Glyndwr
Williams, Richard Owen.

The Dean and Bangor Cathedral Chapter, 1990.

Harold Owen, Arthur Gannon, Richard Jones, Huw Griffith, Michael Preece, Barry Thomas, John F. W. Jones, William Jones, Derek Richards, Wyn Roberts.

Meurig Foulkes, Trevor Evans, Archdeacon Elwyn, Deon Erwyd Edwards, Archdeacon Barry Morgan, Richard Owen, Geraint Vaughan Jones.

Following Bishop Barry's Enthronement, 1993.
Canon John F. W. Jones, Dean Erwyd Edwards, Bishop Barry, Archdeacon Elwyn.

Bishop Barry and the Bangor Cathedral Chapter, 1993.
Alun Hawkins, Dennis Parry, Graham Holland, Michael Preece, Judge David Davies, Arthur Gannon, Gwyndaf Hughes, William Jones, John Lazarus.
Harold Owen, Emyr Rowlands, Margaret Thrall, Geraint Edwards, Eurwyn thomas, Tony Beacon.
Martin Riley, Archdeacon Elwyn, Dean Erwyd Edwards, Bishop Barry, Gareth Lloyd Jones, Archdeacon Saunders Davies, Trevor Evans.

My 65th birthday.

On the *log flume* at
Alton Towers.
Summer 1992.

A pilgrimage to Tŷ Mawr, Wybrnant, 1998.

Parishioners from St David's Church, Glanadda enjoying a picnic
on the pilgrimage.

A day in Ireland, 1996.

The family on Uwchmynydd, overlooking Bardsey Island, 1997.

Our Silver Wedding Anniversary, 1996.

Receiving a gift from the Diocese during the service to celebrate my 40 years in the ministry, 1996.

In the procession at the end of the service.

Erwyd Edwards, Elwyn, Barry Morgan.

Ros, Sioned, Elwyn, Eiflyn, Llinos, Berw.

Ann, John, Ifan, Gwyneth, Basil.

Olwen, Michael, Elwyn, Sian.

Judy, Michael Preece, Elwyn.

Margaret and Eric Clegg, Dorothy Lloyd Lewis, Elwyn, Mair Glyndwr,
Dean Erwyd.
Doreen Hughes, Elen Sytvala, Grace Williams.

Chatting with a few parishioners from Dyffryn Ogwen.

Hilary, Eiflyn, Bethan.

Cutting the cake.

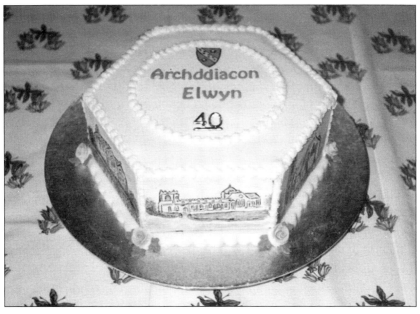

The cake made by Mair Glyndwr, depicting St Michael's College Chapel,
St David's Church, St Tudno's Church, Holy Trinity Church, St Catherine's
Church and Bangor Cathedral.

Celebrating Eiflyn's
mother's 80th birthday.

My Retirement Service at Bangor Cathedral, 1999.

With Saunders and Cynthia. October 1999.

With Cledan and Enid near the Menai Straits.

A few of the Diocesan Office Staff come for tea.
Stella Schultz, Graham Loveluck, Menai Parry, Cathryn Hughes, Dafydd Owen,
Elwyn, Alun Davies.

A visit to the Diocesan Office, 2003.
Stella Schultz, Lorraine Lee, Cathryn Thomas, Eryl Sewell, Elwyn,
Janice ap Thomas.

A visit from Brother Nathanael, 1999.

My 70th birthday.

A visit to Red Wharf Bay. Summer 2002.

A visit from Trevor and Chris, with Bishop John Charles
and the Rev. Willey Okelo from Uganda. Summer 2003.

Don Godber, a former pupil at Friars takes me to see the school as it is today. Summer 2003.

Below:
The family in the garden.

Llinos'
Graduation
day at the
University
of Wales,
College of
Medicine,
Cardiff.
July 1999.

Sioned's
Graduation
day at the
University of
Wales,
Bangor.
July 2003.

A visit from Elwyn and Ann.
Summer 2003.

Right:
A visit to Dr Ohri's clinic. Summer 2003.

Below:
A visit from Dr David Jones.
Summer 2003.

Celebrating my mother's 98th birthday.

Photo: Gwyn Roberts

napter 12

ANADDA 1966-1971

Chapter 12

VICAR OF GLANADDA 1966-1971

The first Vicar of the parish of Glanadda was the Rev. T. Lewis Jones, a man of many parts who left his indelible mark on the newly created parish. He was a keen campanologist and when he came across a skilled ringer he would get him a job on the railway, (which in its heyday employed about a thousand men), and import him to St David's tower. Many of the unusual names on the ringing boards belonged to these "imports".

He was also a hymn writer. The best known of his hymns is probably:

O Arglwydd, dyro nerth
I ddringo'r creigiau serth
   Sydd ar fy nhaith;
Mae'r ffordd yn ddyrys iawn,
A rhwystrau lawer gawn
O foreu hyd brydnawn
   Drwy'r yrfa faith.

– a hymn prompted, it is said, by the steep climb up Penchwintan hill to the Vicarage. He was also a wood carver. Some of his work is still to be seen at the Vicarage, and also a keen and knowledgeable gardener although by now the glory is departed.

Lewis Jones was succeeded by Morgan Jones, then Cybi Jones, Gilbert Wright and myself. I was at first hesitant about moving back to the parish where I had served my first and only curacy. But the principle of better the devil you know than the devil you don't prevailed, and I settled down to my second tour of duty at Glanadda in 1966.

There were two hospitals in the parish, St David's the County Maternity Hospital, and Minffordd which served as the County Isolation Hospital, and I was part time Chaplain to both. As such I would visit regularly, and administer the sacrament and make myself available as required. St David's was an old fashioned building with long wards and ward services were held every Sunday afternoon. The operating theatre was located at the far end of one of these wards – so all the theatre "traffic" trundled in and out of the ward – a procedure that made it difficult to concentrate on the service.

When St David's had a geriatric wing attached to it, the Matron was terribly upset when the obituary notice in the Daily Post included a reference to a person's death "at St David's Hospital". She was afraid that people would conclude from this that medical and nursing standards at "her" hospital had declined!

I found it useful to do my visiting rounds of the hospital at exactly the same time each week. In this way people came to expect you; "Mr Roberts will be here at 3.30." As Chaplain of the Hospital one had pastoral responsibility not only for the patients but also for the whole hospital community. This involved being available at any hour of the day or night, especially to administer Baptism in the case of seriously ill patients who were being transferred for specialist treatment in Liverpool – Walton or Broadgreen Hospitals.

Minffordd was the old "fever" hospital but in my time it was used for convalescence and the treatment of skin diseases. I had to be constantly on guard when I was visiting, not for fear of contracting a skin disease, but for fear of nurses' pranks! There was one occasion when I had left my case, containing my service equipment and robes, in the Sister's office. When I'd finished my rounds, I picked up my case and went on my way to do some calls in the parish. When I opened my case, I found it full of ladies' underwear. I had some difficulty in explaining to my parishioners what it was all about!

There was also a V.C. School in the parish – Vaynol School in

Penrhosgarnedd. The Headmaster was William Pritchard to whom I referred earlier. Like most villages at the time, much of the community's life revolved around the headmaster and the village school. The school building was in very poor condition – so poor that the old building was replaced by a new school building in 1954. As Incumbent of the parish I was ex-officio Chairman of the Governors, as I was to become later in the case of St George's School in Llandudno. Like many old schools which were replaced by new ones, many parishes thought that the obsolete school buildings were now the property of the parish. This was not so and the misunderstanding caused a lot of unease and bitterness in the parishes who felt that they were being deprived of what was rightfully theirs.

Glanadda was never a rich parish and in addition to meeting day to day running costs like any other parish, it had the debt on the new St Peter's to pay off. Consequently there were regular money raising efforts to meet the bills and I'm glad to say that St David's enthusiastically took part. It was a case of "Bear ye one another's burdens".

Many of the regular money raising efforts were evening mystery trips and a Men's Evening. These were sometimes hilarious especially when things went wrong, as they often did. I remember one occasion when one of the men stood behind the stage curtain with a telephone directory and another in front of the curtain with an identical Directory. The point was to give a demonstration of mind reading – someone would choose a number and the clairvoyant would transmit to the other. Unfortunately the receiver was rather hard of hearing and burst out, "Shout, I can't hear you!" These were happy social occasions as well as money raising efforts.

Another duty assigned to me while I was in Glanadda was Director of Post Ordination Training and Non-stipendiary ministry. Bishop Gwilym with remarkable vision foresaw the time coming, and that soon, when we would have to revise our familiar pattern of ordained ministry and make provision for the ordination of older men, (women were not ordained at that stage), who would be ordained while continuing in their secular work. They would serve alongside their stipendiary colleagues in the parishes in which they lived. This development was viewed with suspicion by many who regarded this as a back door to ordination. There were four in the first batch who offered their services to serve in this way, and the quality of their ministry soon allayed these suspicions. We devised a diocesan training course, based on a tutorial system and I am very proud to have been involved in the development of this ministry in which the Diocese of Bangor led the way for the Province as in so many other things. Although there were some who regarded it as a back door to ordination, the quality of the first generation soon silenced the critics. Indeed this ministry is now so well established that one wonders what the fuss was all about.

Among that small pioneering group were R. M. Jones who worked with Manweb, G. I. Jones a schoolteacher from Llangefni, R. Lewis Edwards a schoolmaster, R. E. Thomas who was Manager of Boots the Chemist and then there was Robert Williams, a schoolmaster at Marian-glas, Anglesey. He had come to live in Bangor in retirement. He was ordained to serve in the parish of Glanadda with Penrhosgarnedd and no one could have wished for a more loyal colleague or devoted priest.

St David's Vicarage is one of the most attractive houses in the Diocese and far too big for occupation by a single person. However Susie Rowlands, one of the parishioners in Glanadda looked after me as a housekeeper and took great pride in her position. She would come early in the morning when it was still dark so that she would not be seen making her way to the Vicarage, although it was an open secret that she acted as my housekeeper. I couldn't see what there was to be secretive about. Like Richard Hughes in Pentir days her grasp of English was not good and she often got her English words mis-pronounced. She would sometimes ask me to pick something up in town. I remember one occasion when she asked me to bring some, what sounded like Carnicle Red Polish. All the shopkeepers I asked looked blank at me until one realised that what I was looking for was Cardinal Red Polish! Even though Susie didn't quite know the correct name, she knew how to use the polish and Glanadda Vicarage sparkled in her care.

People may well think that a cleric's life is dull and unexciting but that is not so. Amusing things happen even in the most unexpected of places. I was once conducting the marriage ceremony of a very nervous couple. Having carefully guided them through the first part of the service, with whispered directions as we went along, we needed to move up to the altar for the second part. I whispered to the couple to follow me but hearing a shuffling noise behind me I turned round to see what was going on and to my amazement found the couple on their knees shuffling along after me!

My own marriage was soon to follow. In the Spring of 1971, I told the Bishop my intention of becoming engaged. It was agreed that that would be a convenient time to start a new life together in a new parish, so I was officially appointed Rector of Llandudno. Little did I realise that I was also about to become one of Marks and Spencer's best customers!

Chapter 13

RECTOR OF LLANDUDNO 1971-1983

The Llandudno we know today as a holiday resort and shopping centre is largely the creation of Mostyn Estates and Owen Williams, a Liverpool architect. The town is situated on the Creuddyn Peninsula with two splendid headlands, the Great Orme and Little Orme. The flatland between the headlands was a saltmarsh which was transformed into the Llandudno of today.

This area we know as Llandudno is divided into two ecclesiastical parishes – Llandudno and Llanrhos, and those parishes are in different dioceses – "our" Llandudno in the Diocese of Bangor, and Llanrhos, the easterly side of the town, in the Diocese of St Asaph. The story begins with St Tudno, one of the early Celtic saints who established his cell on the Great Orme in the 7th Century. This later became St Tudno's Church but in a storm in 1839 the roof was blown off and the church was left a virtual ruin until 1855 when it was repaired. Open air services are held there now, during the Summer months.

The Parish Church of St George was built in 1840 at the foot of the Great Orme. However it soon proved to be too small to accommodate the growing number of visitors to the town. This increase had been due to the completion of the main line railway system between Llandudno and Llandudno Junction in 1858. Unfortunately, due to the cost of maintenance St George's Church was closed at the end of 2002.

The Church of Holy Trinity was built in 1874 on an imposing site in the centre of the town, on land donated by Lady Mostyn. This Church which was much larger and more central than the Parish Church was built to accommodate the growing population and increase in visitors at that time. With the closure of St George's Church, Holy Trinity Church has now become the Parish Church.

St Beuno's Church was the old Orme School and it served the close knit community of the Great Orme. It had been leased from Mostyn Estates but it ceased to be a church a few years ago. At one time there was a corrugated iron structure in the Trinity Avenue area known as St Andrew's Church, whose memory is preserved in street names such as St Andrew's Avenue and St Andrew's Place. Originally this church was in Llanrhos Parish.

In 1911 the Church of our Saviour was built in the West Shore. This was a community Church with fine facilities which replaced St Andrew's. This has now been leased to the English Baptist Church.

As a popular and busy resort, Llandudno attracted a regular clientele of visitors and holiday makers. The memories of happy holidays then led many to settle there when retirement came. At first all would go well, but eventually one of the partners died and the survivor would be left high and dry – another name added to a list of lonely people to be ministered to. There are many people who are not involved in the holiday industry apart from finding parking spaces in the height of summer.

I found two types of retired people – those who have all the time in the world to do the things they want to do, and the other – "I'm retired now so I don't really want to do anything". A first class example was Bill Harris, who battled bravely against illness yet was the first to offer his services to any task that needed doing.

I arrived at Llandudno at the height of the holiday season and for the first few months I saw more visitors than I did parishioners. The Rectory was situated near St George's Church, in Church Walks.

While I was Vicar of Glanadda, I had got engaged to Eiflyn the elder daughter of Griffith John Roberts, the late Vicar of Conwy, and Margaret Morris Roberts and we arranged our wedding for

October 16th 1971 at Holy Trinity Church, with the Bishop conducting the service. My brother Basil was at sea when we were married so our best man was Dr Elwyn Roberts, (this caused a great deal of confusion as we both had the same name). Eiflyn was given away by her Uncle Richard and the bridesmaids were Olwen (Eiflyn's sister), Judith (school friend) and young attendants Bethan and Berwyn. Our ushers were Ifan (Gwyneth's husband), John (my first cousin) and Stephen (Eiflyn's Cousin) It was for us a memorable occasion, marred by one sad event. My Churchwarden at Glanadda, Mr Billy Lane was one of the guests at the wedding. He was a keen amateur photographer and when he got home he started processing the photos he had taken. No sooner had he finished that he suffered a heart attack and died. "In the midst of life we are in death."

Eiflyn gave up teaching at Maelgwn School in Llandudno Junction to manage the large Rectory that we lived in and to help with any voluntary work in the parish, as did many other parishioners. At that time there were seven Sunday services in four of the Churches and when the summer months came, there was an additional open air service at St Tudno's Church on the Great Orme. Mattins and Evensong were held daily at Holy Trinity Church. Even though some of the parishioners spoke Welsh, the church services were held in English, except for weekday Mattins and Evensong.

It was during our time in Llandudno that our two daughters were born. Llinos Gwawr was born at St David's Hospital, Bangor on 12th July 1976. It seems that for a baby to be born at the Rectory was a rare event. To celebrate her birth, a peal of bells was rung at Holy Trinity Church. Llinos was christened in September at St George's Church by Bishop Gwilym who was by then Archbishop of Wales. Sioned Eleri was born at the Maelor Hospital, Wrexham on 2nd April 1982. She was also christened by Bishop Gwilym at St George's Church in July and the parish shared in our joy once again when all the congregation joined our family for refreshments in the Rectory Garden after the service.

Llandudno is a Rectorial Benefice and under the Regulations of the Church in Wales, provision is made for the following staff: Rector, Vicar, Assistant Curate and NSM. My first Vicar and colleague was the Reverend Trevor Evans who was already in post. His knowledge and experience of the parish were invaluable in settling me in. And the cheerful and jovial nature of the Reverend Geraint Edwards, the Assistant Curate, lightened many dark moments. As I noted earlier R. Evans Thomas was one of the first in the Province of Wales to serve in the Non Stipendiary Ministry. When he retired from Boots the Chemist he became virtually a full time member of the parish staff. In him we saw the NSM at its best. We also benefited from the ministry of clergy who had retired and come to live in Llandudno and also Franciscan Friars from the Franciscan House that was in the parish of Llanrhos.

Many immigrants from England never grasped that the Church in Wales is not an established church like the Church of England but an independent Province of the Anglican Communion. So the Church in Wales was treated as the Church of England and Holy Trinity because of its size and central location was regarded as a Civic Church. The Rector was automatically the one who was invited to conduct special services – civic services, Remembrance Day services, blessing a new lifeboat and many other such occasions.

There were also invitations to do a short religious slot in the band concerts on a Sunday evening – the only place where I was applauded after a sermon. I'm not sure if it was a recognition of the excellence of the sermon or relief that it was finished! I also served as Chaplain to the Actors' Church Union which involved visiting the various theatres in the town (Arcadia, Pier, Grand), making oneself known to the artistes and being available when problems arose. The entertainment profession is a precarious business and it is surprising how many artistes who are outwardly without a care in the world, are inwardly deeply unhappy. Thanks to the co-operation of people like Gwen Overton and Clive Stock and Wyn Calvin (whose brother was a

Presbyterian Minister in Llandudno), we usually had a service at Holy Trinity to round off the summer season.

Weekdays were taken up with visiting, funerals, appointments for arranging weddings and Society meetings. There were two branches of the Mothers' Union, the Churchwomen's Fellowship, Young Wives, the Men's Society, and the Girls' Friendly Society. A Play School was held at the Church of our Saviour Hall and later a Mother and Toddler Group at Holy Trinity Church Hall. Both were the brainchild of Chris, Trevor's wife. All these Societies would cease to hold their meetings in May as regular parishioners became more involved with the holiday trade.

Although not technically in our parish, a Franciscan House was established in the old Llanrhos Vicarage, and we were in on the initial planning. It was a memorable evening at the Rectory when three Friars – Brother Michael, Brother Silyn and Brother Nathanael stayed with us to work out the details of the proposed new house and their future ministry in Llandudno. The old Vicarage in Llanrhos was renamed Tŷ'r Brodyr (the Friary) and over the years housed many other Friars. Franciscan Friars follow the ideals of St. Francis of Assisi and to this day they are active in missionary work all over the world.

The holiday season brought with it a regular crop of problem people who took advantage of the anonymity of a holiday situation to unburden themselves on those they would be unlikely to meet again. Some of these were victims of circumstances such as grief after the death of a partner that made one break up a home and take to the road, while some were out and out rogues. "I need to get to my mother in hospital. I'll pay you back when my benefit comes through", were familiar words. Sadly we heard this too often. Sometimes we believed it and gave money only to discover the same person wandering the streets late that night, blind drunk. Sometimes the story was true, but how could we tell? We made a rule not to give money but to provide some basic food. We had an arrangement with the Roman Catholic Church to offer food vouchers, as part of our scheme. The Franciscan Brothers would also help in this way by giving some wayfarers a bed for the night.

An example of a rogue who descended on us was one who called himself Lord David Hey, who turned up at the Annual Fête one year, claiming to be a distant relative of the Queen and who had fallen on evil days, and he produced photos to prove his claim. He claimed to be trying to get back to Scotland to join his family. I took him to the station, bought him a single ticket to whatever station he'd said, and heaved a sigh of relief as the train left. I hadn't been home long when I received a phone call from the police, "We've got a friend of yours here who has been taken off the train because he was stone drunk! Shall we send him back to you?" My response was "You dare!" and that mercifully was the last I heard of him. We later found that he'd tried the same ploy on the Methodist Minister in Llandudno. (He most probably had provided him with the money which he used to purchase drink.)

Different, yet equally demanding, if not more so, was the case of M, a young epileptic from Yorkshire, who wanted to prove that she could stand on her own feet by taking up a casual holiday job. When this was too much for her, she landed in the Rectory one day. We were given a clearance by her doctor to call an ambulance to transfer her to hospital when these fits occurred. Eventually she decided to return home and with another sigh of relief we put her on the train. Believe it or not, within a fortnight she was back again and once again we started on the same merry-go-round. One couldn't help admiring her courage and determination. She is now married to a priest and they have five children. Despite continuous ill health she copes and we still keep in touch.

Another unexpected guest that landed on us at the Rectory was a Canadian priest who had been taken ill when on a visit to some relatives in Ruthin. I came into the picture when I had a phone call from Llandudno Hospital, (although the hospital was technically in Llanrhos Parish), asking me to go over to minister to him and his wife. Eventually he rallied and the time came when he could be discharged from hospital and the question arose where was he going to be discharged to. He was in no fit state to face a journey to Canada and the relative he had come to visit lived in Ruthin. So the net closed in on Llandudno Rectory. In the meantime members of his family began to converge on Llandudno and they almost took over the Rectory – mowing the lawn, taking the dog for a walk, even opening the front door to visitors! Every time I passed the Canon's bedroom he would waylay me and start some story which seemed never ending. So every time I passed his room, I put on my cassock, on the pretext of getting ready for a funeral – "Sorry I'm on my way to a funeral. Tell me about it later."

Before long we felt that they were outstaying their welcome and yet there was no mention of what plans they had about going home. I eventually told them that the Parsonage Board had arranged for some woodworm eradication work to be carried out in the Rectory. A few days later we bade them farewell with a sigh of relief. The Canon lived for another five years, and his widow still keeps in touch with us.

While I was Rector of Llandudno I attended a mid service training course at St George's House Conference Centre in Windsor Castle. The course lasted a month and consisted of lectures and visits to parishes in the neighbourhood. We were all required to prepare a project before the course commenced which was later presented to other colleagues for discussion. My subject was the Non Stipendiary Ministry in the Church in Wales. The climax was a question and answer session with Archbishop Michael Ramsey, clearly a man of deep spirituality and of great pastoral warmth. It was an unforgettable experience.

We shared in the life of the Castle community and were given access to parts of the castle not normally open to the public. St George's is the Chapel of the Knights of the Garter. I was allocated a stall belonging to the Emperor of Japan. I am not sure if this was an honour for him or for me! We were present for the funeral of a minor member of the Royal family and we saw at first hand how meticulous are the preparations for events such as these.

For most of my time as Rector of Llandudno, my Rector's Warden was O. E. Lloyd Jones, a formidable figure who served the Church well at provincial, diocesan as well as parish level. Yet beneath this rather formidable exterior there beat a heart of gold. He judged everything by financial success. I remember him asking me just before some conference service at Holy Trinity, (of which we had many each summer), "Is this a proper service?" As it was a special service, drawn up specially for this conference, I thought he was being sarcastic and I responded rather sharply, "What do you mean? Of course it's a proper service." "Well," he replied, "is there a collection in it?" He had a dry sense of humour. He once told me, "I've got bad news for you. My sister is coming to live in the parish!" Mary was very similar to her brother in appearance and temperament.

His fellow Warden Charles Jones was a very different character, a very shy and retiring person yet a very active and efficient organiser of the annual parish Garden Fête. Holy Trinity Hall was small so when the Annual Garden Fête was held in July it had been a custom for the Fête Organiser to hire an enormous marquee. More often than not it was a sweltering hot day. The Fête was usually opened by a famous entertainer, who was appearing at what was then the Arcadia Theatre. Following Charles Jones' retirement, responsibility for organising the Fête was taken by Bill Harris and Ken Hind. It was always an exhausting but pleasurable event, but gave me a chance to meet visitors, many of whom had already attended a service the previous Sunday.

Another unique character was Harry Geeson. He was a throwback from palmier days and one of the few, if any, "full time vergers" employed by an "ordinary parish church". He was tremendously pleased when the Bishop said to him after a Confirmation service, "Take care of yourself Mr Geeson. I can always get a Rector for Llandudno, but good vergers are very hard to find."

He knew exactly where everything was kept in church, where every screw of the Crib was kept, and year after year they would emerge from their hiding places to do duty for another year. His watchword in the face of any impending change was "It's been the same for 'undreds of years!"

There was one occasion when Trevor and I decided to check the chairs in Holy Trinity for woodworm and to throw out those which were badly infected. The chairs left behind seemed to be getting no fewer until we realised that for every chair that went out Harry Geeson brought one back in.

Another noteable character was Edward Jones a member of St Beuno's Church. He was also our gravedigger who in addition to his duties looked after St Tudno's Church and the surrounding cemetery. He knew the location of every grave in the Churchyard. There are many vaults in St Tudno's Churchyard and Edward's knowledge of who was buried where surpassed any record books or computers.

At the pier end of the Promenade lived a larger than life character, an interesting lady named Elsie Partington. She was in her element entertaining theatrical visitors and like a lady bountiful supported all good causes. I can't recall seeing her in Church but she held an open house from time to time to which we were invited and she was generous in her hospitality. Every time the Lifeboat was launched on a service, there would always be a bottle of whisky awaiting the weary crew on their return.

I also had my moments with the Lifeboat. A request had been received by the Lifeboat Secretary for a burial at sea and I was asked to conduct it. We decided on a date and time and decided to combine the burial with an exercise which the Lifeboat was required to carry out at regular intervals. The only snag here was that I had to be back at Holy Trinity Church to meet the Archbishop who was to preach at a Christingle service later that afternoon. So it was arranged that I should go out in the big boat, conduct the committal service and then be transferred to the inshore boat and that would bring me back to shore while the big boat went off to continue its exercise. More for the sake of saying something than to seek information, I asked the crew, "How fast does this boat go?" to which they replied, "Hang on. We'll show you!" At the touch of a button, the boat shot forward and I was delivered to Holy Trinity looking like a drowned rat to meet the Archbishop!

On the day that I was to be installed as Chancellor of Bangor Cathedral I decided to take the afternoon off by going with the family to the Fairground at Colwyn Bay. We had a go on a few rides and ended up on an electric train which went round and round in a figure of eight. Trade was rather slow and only Llinos, Eiflyn and myself were on the ride. The operator took our money, pressed some switches and off went the electric train. Meanwhile the operator who had clearly been having a go at some strong liquor disappeared round the corner while the infernal machine went round and round and there seemed to be no obvious escape. I had visions of a full Cathedral waiting for the star of the show to appear.

When Archbishop Glyn Simon invited me to be a member of the newly formed Church in Wales Doctrinal Commission, he said that he didn't anticipate that the work involved would be too arduous and time consuming, even with the responsibilities of a large parish like Llandudno! In fact we found that a constant flow of work required our attention.

The first Convenor of the Doctrinal Commission was Dr Greville Yarnold and under his benign yet penetrating leadership, we soon became an effective and hard working group. When I was invited to succeed Greville as Convener I felt highly honoured and privileged

Lady Mostyn could not have foreseen years ago the problems that donating land in such a central position could cause. During the summer we seemed to spend more time keeping cars out than allowing cars in. Instructive and interesting were the "offenders'" excuses when caught – "Canon Rowlands gave me permission", but he died 30 years ago! One conscientious Churchwarden, Ken Docksey, challenged a person who had just parked his car in the grounds and who offered by way of explanation – "I am a friend of the Rector's." To which the Warden responded, "Oh yes, they all say that". He was in fact my best man!

It was always a joy in the summer months to be conducting a service at the ancient church of Saint Tudno that is situated on the Great Orme. The local bus company always arranged a shuttle service to bring people up from town. As the church itself was so small, this was an open air service and it was not unusual on a fine Sunday morning to have an attendance of between 300 and 800, visitors and locals. Some people would sit along the cemetery wall and hill – popularly known as Aberdeen Hill because it was within range of the service but out of range of the collection! I often thought it seemed like the crowd one would imagine in the Sermon on the Mount.

Twice a year a few faithful parishioners would meet at Holy Trinity grounds and be transported up the Orme to give the church a good clean, during May just before the first Service on Whitsunday and then in September for the Harvest Festival. It was 'bring your own brushes and mops' but what memorable occasions they were. The cleaning was always followed by tea at The Rectory Tea Gardens nearby – free of charge. A few years back we got into a bit of confusion over the Whitsun week-end. Whitsun had been the Sunday on which our services started for the season but an adjustment to the calendar detached the Christian Whitsun from the secular Bank Holiday. We had arranged a service for what was in the Church Calendar and that was that. Then shortly before lunch, a dozen people called at the Rectory to explain that they had gone to St Tudno's church expecting a service but as no cleric turned up, they had conducted their own service and had come to hand over the collection. Everyone understood how the confusion had occurred and we all learnt a lesson for the future.

My sermons have always been short and to the point I hope, but I must admit that I was uneasy at times in the summer months when preaching to about 500 people in Holy Trinity Church. It is one thing to know your parishioners well, it is another thing to wonder how many Church dignitaries from other parts of the country are in the congregation. I shall always remember being told once, "If you notice a male holiday-maker wearing black shoes in the congregation you can be certain that he is a Bishop in disguise." It was surprising though how many men wore black shoes!

Our parishioners were hard working and eager to venture on any new activities. Many money raising events developed into popular social gatherings, events such as Strawberry Teas, Welsh Teas and Pancake Teas. There was one particular Shrove Tuesday when we had been invited to join two of our parishioners for a meal that evening at a Restaurant up the Conwy Valley. We still remember that on the menu for that evening there was Creamed fish in Pancakes for the first course and Pancakes with Maple Syrup for the dessert. Needless to say, having cooked and served over 200 pancakes in the Church hall that afternoon, the last thing we wanted to eat that particular evening was Pancakes!!

We were fortunate that as a family we were in Llandudno at a time when there were other clergy and wives with young children. The Vicarage family when we moved to the parish were Trevor, Chris and their children Simon and Ruth. Trevor moved to Llanidloes in 1975 and was succeeded by Berw, Ros and their children, at that time Mark, Trystan and Angharad. Dyfan and Gwynan were born after the family moved to live in Penmaenmawr. Berw's down to earth approach in the parish was greatly appreciated. Those were the days when there were more clergy in the various deaneries and Arllechwedd Deanery seemed to have many young families. So every so often all the families would join for a picnic, walk or some other activity. Nowadays there are fewer clergy in the deaneries, far more grouped parishes and so families live further away from each other

Early in 1983 the Venerable H. A. Evans, Archdeacon of Bangor, retired and the Venerable Tom Bayley Hughes, then Archdeacon of Merioneth was appointed in his place and I was appointed to fill the vacancy in the Southern Archdeaconry. My appointment was to be announced on Easter Day and the Reverend R. E. Thomas, our Non Stipendiary Minister at Llandudno, "kind and thoughtful man that he was", offered to make the announcement for me at the main Morning Service. So Dick made the announcement that I had been appointed Archdeacon of Merioneth and that I would shortly be leaving Llandudno to take up my new appointment. He then proceeded to announce the next hymn which was:

"The strife is o'er, the battle done"!

Chapter 14

WHAT IS AN ARCHDEACON?

It is impossible to provide a detailed and generally accurate description of the activities of an Archdeacon, since his office is in essence that of assisting the Bishop in the exercise of his episcopate and different Bishops might require different things of their Archdeacon.

Originally the Archdeacon was the chief of the deacons who assisted the Bishop in his work, and this close connection is reflected in the Ordinal where it is the Bishop alone who lays hands on the candidate. It has been said that the Bishop is a 'cuddly, friendly Labrador' and the Archdeacon is 'the Rottweiler', but most Archdeacons speak or prefer to speak of their role as pastor and friend.

An old title is 'oculus episcopi – bishop's eye' although some might render it 'bishop's spy'! In mediaeval time he was very much concerned with business and disciplinary matters, so much so that it was the subject of serious theological debate ' can an Archdeacon be saved?'

There are three main parts to an Archdeacon's job, and the most straightforward is the part that relates to the care of Church buildings. Working with the Diocesan Advisory Committee, Archdeacons manage the progress of applications, whether these concern installing modern facilities, or reordering pews or an altar for liturgical purposes. This Committee does not grant the faculty. This is done by the Chancellor who can grant or with-hold faculty. The Archdeacon's Certificate or Minor Faculty no longer exists. There is sometimes a tension between the organizations like Cadw and the liturgical insights of a parish.

We weigh the care of the ancient fabric against adapting churches for use by a living church.

In addition to the administrative authority delegated to him by the Bishop in part of the Diocese, the Archdeacon has a legal and judicial function as laid down in the *Constitution of the Church in Wales*. He admits Churchwardens to office at the Annual Visitation and inspects the documents required of them. This provides an opportunity for parishes to bring forward any matters which they feel need to be brought to the attention of the Bishop. This is also an opportunity for pastoral and personal contact. The Bishop is officially responsible for pastoral matters, but these are often delegated to Archdeacons at least in the initial stages.

Chapter 15

ARCHDEACON OF MERIONETH
AND RECTOR OF CRICCIETH 1983-1986

The Archdeaconry of Merioneth has contributed richly to the cultural life of Wales. It was in this Archdeaconry that one of our most famous Churchmen carried out his ministry. Edmwnd Prys was ordained priest in 1568, served in the Parish of Maentwrog and later became Archdeacon of Merioneth. A renowned poet, he composed *Salmau Cân*, which are metrical Psalms and our first Hymn Book. These are still sung in many Churches and Chapels to this day.

In addition to the duties of Archdeacon I also had responsibility for the parish of Criccieth with Treflys. This arrangement had its advantages and disadvantages. The advantages were that you shared with your fellow clerics in the joys and sorrows of parish life. One faced the same problems that they did. The disadvantage was that you became a split personality as you tried to do justice to two jobs.

Almost all I knew about Criccieth before we went there was that it was the home of the delicious Cadwaladr Ice Cream, but we soon found that there was more to it than that. It was in many ways a 'mini' Llandudno, having developed as a holiday resort on the Cambrian Coast in the late Victorian era.

The ancient parish Church of Saint Catherine is just a stone's throw from the Church of Saint Deiniol, built as the English Church during Criccieth's heyday as a holiday resort. It has now been sold and converted into flats.

Saint Michael's Church Treflys is situated on the hillside overlooking Morfa Bychan. The only items of liturgical interest are inscribed stones similar to early Christian inscribed stones at Penmachno.

The Archdeaconry of Merioneth covers the Southern part of the Diocese of Bangor from Llŷn and Eifionydd in the North to Arwystli in the South, so the people of the Southern Deanery are nearer to the Cathedrals of Brecon and Hereford than they are to their own. This tends to militate against an awareness of diocesan unity, and the Archdeaconry serves as a more manageable unit.

Prior to my appointment as Archdeacon I had never served in the Archdeaconry of Merioneth, so I had to learn a new job and also find my way around unfamiliar territory, and I can't thank the good people of Merioneth enough for the help, encouragement and support which they gave to a new boy.

One of the new experiences that I got involved with as Archdeacon of Merioneth was the Plygain, which is well established in the southern parishes of the Archdeaconry. The word Plygain comes from the Latin "pulli cantus" which means the 'cockerel's crow' and the Mallwyd/Llanerfyl region has always been renowned for this traditional service since the early 17th Century. Carols are preserved in families and passed on through generations. There is no prearranged order of service but people, either as individuals or parties, come forward to sing. The carols usually have many long verses and are usually sung unaccompanied.

An authority on the Plygain services when I was Archdeacon in Merioneth was Canon Geraint Vaughan Jones, who sadly died a few months ago. I asked him once if he had any untoward experience with the Plygain and he replied, "No, no real trouble, but on one occasion, a mother and her child came forward, with a guitar, to sing "Rudolph the Red Nosed Reindeer", and in the second half of the service they came forward again but this time to sing "Jingle Bells!"

One of the first lessons I learnt was that the duties of an Archdeacon are many and varied. One morning I had a phone call from an irate woman, complaining that the goats from the Vicarage garden which adjoined hers, had broken loose and eaten her prize azaleas. "And what are you going to do about it?" was her challenging parting shot. What I said or did to calm the storm I forget now, but the incident brought home to me that as an Archdeacon I would have to get ready for anything!

It was impossible for us to move into the Rectory prior to my Induction, because so much substantial improvement work had to be carried out. So we were housed temporarily in one of the two bungalows which Sir Billy Butlin had given to the Church in Wales, for the use of Retired Clergy and Widows. This state of affairs lasted for five months. Despite the difficult circumstances everyone made an effort to make us feel at home.

Another complication in our move was that the children had just contracted Chicken Pox and were too poorly to be brought to the Induction Service which we held at St. Catherine's on July 29th 1983.

The Rectory Close at Criccieth was well peppered with ecclesiastical dignitaries of various kinds. There was Mrs Lemuel Jones the widow of Canon Lemuel T. Jones and Canon and Mrs Ken Francis who occupied the second of the Butlins Bungalows; then the Archdeacon/Rector at the Rectory, and next to the garden was the home of the retired Archbishop of Wales, Bishop Gwilym. Some people found it difficult to get on with him, feeling that the Headmaster was not far from the surface, but I always found him kind and helpful.

When we went away on holiday, he was the keeper of the goldfish until one evening the phone rang and a sheepish voice came over: "Gwilym here, I'm afraid one of the goldfish has died". A couple of days later this scenario was repeated and that was the last time he was invited to look after our livestock. Skilled fisherman that he was, he met his match with our couple of goldfish.

I shall always remember the first service I took at Treflys and my dismay at finding that there were only two people in the congregation. Pretty soon the Church of St Michael's experienced something of a revival, which was nothing of my doing. Situated on the hillside of Morfa Bychan it was technically in the parish of Porthmadoc but for all practical purposes it went with Criccieth. As the new housing estate there reached completion and people started to move into their new homes, word got around that they had discovered a little church which held services in English, (it was the language that attracted them, not any denominationalism) and the congregation grew from two to two dozen. Although I doubt if any of them had heard of the Constitution of the Church in Wales, Emmerson and Bobbie Carley were elected Wardens, Peggy Graveson became our conscientious Organist and in due course, with their aid and the rest of the congregation, we reached the heights of a Carol Service and the Church was full.

However people died as well as lived in Treflys and we had to make provision for an extension to the graveyard. A date was agreed with the Bishop – J. C. Mears – but alas when the appointed day came, there was a heavy fall of snow and only the Bishop and I managed to get through to consecrate the new churchyard. The ceremonial for the blessing of a churchyard requires the Bishop and Incumbent to process around the new section. So the Bishop and I trudged around the new churchyard area in a scene reminiscent of Good King Wenceslas.

For many years the Pathfinders' movement had held their summer camps in Criccieth and their Sunday services at St Deiniol's Church attracted enthusiastic congregations. They reminded us of the Beach Mission in Llandudno.

There was a happy spirit of co-operation between the various denominations in Criccieth and the various churches all got on well together, with everyone supporting each other's events. St Catherine's always held an Annual Fête, weather permitting, in the Rectory Garden. It was during the preparation for one particular Fête that we all experienced one of the most frightening earth tremors that were prevalent at that time. We often wonder if those tremors had been the cause of the Rectory having to be re-roofed a few years later.

Just as Eiflyn and I were brought up in a Vicarage, so Llinos and Sioned joined with us in many Parish events. They both attended Sunday Schools in all the parishes and took it in turns with others to be Mary, Gabriel, a King or a Shepherd. I can thankfully say that neither of them called "Dad" or tried to come to me in any service that I was conducting, simply because they brought along their crayons, colouring books and biscuits and kept themselves amused.

But bad habits can sometimes land you in trouble, as we discovered to our embarrassment at my God daughter Kate's wedding in Wimbledon. Both the girls were bridesmaids. Llinos was then aged eight and responsible enough to care for her little sister, but there was no way of knowing what Sioned would get up to at the tender age of two! When all were seated for the short address, Sioned walked down the aisle, swinging her basket of flowers and when she reached our pew, she whispered, "Biscuit please!" Fortunately Eiflyn had come prepared and gave her one. When bride, groom and bridesmaids were up at the altar, we had a repeat performance but this time the request was, "A biscuit for Llinos please"! Needless to say, they both stole the show.

It has always been a joke in our family when going on outings that according to Llinos and Sioned, "We can't take you anywhere Dad. There's always someone who knows you, wherever we go"! It was while we were in Criccieth that both the girls won a Fancy Dress Competition and the prize was a trip on the little train from Porthmadoc to Blaenau Ffestiniog and back. Father Christmas would also be on the train to meet children and hand them a small gift each. When he came to our seats, he looked at me and in a loud voice shouted, "I remember you! You were preaching Harvest in Blaenau Ffestiniog recently!" Believe me, it was difficult to explain this to the girls!

It was during our time in Criccieth in 1984 that problems with my health came to light. I knew that all wasn't well. I was constantly tired and I found that things which I normally enjoyed were becoming more burdensome. After a series of tests at our local hospital, no one seemed able to pinpoint the problem. Eventually Bishop Gwilym, our next door neighbour, persuaded me to go to St Luke's Hospital for the Clergy in London, for a consultation. St Luke's Hospital is a private hospital and it is staffed by eminent consultants who give their services free as a token of their gratitude to the church for services rendered. It was there that tests, including a brain scan, were carried out. I returned home and had to wait one week for the results, which I received from the local GP in Criccieth. I was diagnosed as having Parkinson's Disease, a progressive illness for which there is no cure.

When we first received the news, our first reaction was shock and even horror. That evening it was difficult to conduct the Harvest Thanksgiving service at St. Catherine's Church, followed by a Harvest Supper for over one hundred parishioners. It was during the early hours of the morning that we shared our thoughts and eventually decided to take a more positive approach and deal with the disease as a foe to be overcome.

I was fortunate enough to be put in the care of Dr Andrew Lees, a Neurological Consultant at the Middlesex Hospital, London, and an international authority on Parkinson's Disease. Parkinson sufferers are all different, and the rate of deterioration varies from person to person. Even though there is as yet no cure, there are many drugs which alleviate the problems that may arise – especially during the early stages. When I began to feel the benefit of drugs prescribed by Dr Lees, I lived in the hope that I would be able to continue my ministry for as long as possible. We also felt that the best way to combat the disease would be to put up a fight, not keep it a secret and be grateful for small mercies. In a curious way there is relief in knowing what one is up against. There is no point in moaning about your lot – you just have to get on with it.

Chapter 16

ARCHDEACON OF BANGOR 1986-1999

Following the retirement of Archdeacon Tom Bayley Hughes, Bishop Cledan invited me to take up the Archdeaconry of Bangor. I have always maintained that any so called promotion in the Church is not part of some honours system but an appointment to do a job of work, and it was with that understanding that I accepted the Bishop's appointment to Bangor in 1986. So once again, the Roberts household was on the move.

The Archdeaconry of Bangor consists of the whole of Anglesey and the old County of Caernarfon with parts of Merioneth. The house was in Trefonwys, on the outskirts of Bangor – not a good family house or convenient office. When I first moved in, there was no study or office and one of the bedrooms doubled up as a study. I can see even now the astonished looks of my visitors when I invited them to step upstairs! But it did have the advantage of being within convenient distance of the railway station which almost became my second house during my time in Bangor. I made so many journeys to Cardiff that the clerk in the ticket office automatically reached for the correct ticket before I had the chance to ask for it! Then when we arrived in Cardiff, the quick dash to 39 Cathedral Road to work through the afternoon's agenda before an equally quick dash to Cardiff station to get a train back to Bangor. At the end of a long day the fluorescent lights around the Plaza were a very welcome sight indeed.

One practical word of warning – never wear a clerical collar on the London to Holyhead train. By the time you approach

Chester the hard drinking travellers have become very amicable and sing the praises of their fellow travellers and one longs for the train to reach Prestatyn by which time they have fallen asleep!

As the Archdeacon of Bangor has no parochial responsibilities it has been our custom for some years for him to take over much of the committee work, both Diocesan and Provincial. Provincial meetings involve regular visits to Shrewsbury or Cardiff. The Representative Body, based in Cardiff, is largely a formal body and most of its work is done through these committees: Property Sub-committee, Churches' Committee, Provincial Standing Committee. The principle of representation requires that each diocese be represented on each of these committees. Unfortunately most of these meetings are held in Cardiff, sometimes Shrewsbury, which involves the northern representatives in a disproportionate amount of travelling. Travelling backwards and forwards between Bangor and Cardiff in one day, sometimes twice a week, is a wearing business and looking back, I doubt if it was wise to attempt it. Bishop Gwilym used to say that the distance between Cardiff and Bangor was the same as between Bangor and Cardiff, but unfortunately he failed to convince the Southern members of this. The full R.B. after an overnight stay at one of the more fashionable hotels in Llandudno used to have an occasional meeting in the resort starting with an Eucharist at 8 a.m. in Holy Trinity Church before commencing their meetings. The congregation at the Eucharist was once rather sparse. Bishop Gwilym who was the Celebrant then, drew attention to this with the comment, "Not many have come to church this morning, have they?" This comment was picked up by the very sensitive microphone by the altar and the attendance was much better the following day!

There are also several charities, both provincial and diocesan which involve the R.B. An example of the former is the Isla Johnston Trust. This is a benefaction from the sale of Bryn-mêl, Miss Johnston's home at Glyn-garth, Anglesey. During her lifetime it was used for retreats and Quiet Days. It was her wish that it would be used as a retreat house for the Church in Wales, but after her death this proved to be impracticable, and after prolonged negotiation with various bodies it has now ended up as a private Nursing Home. The proceeds of sale now fund the Isla Johnston Trust, which is a wide ranging trust.

The Bishop Henry Rowlands Charity is another example amongst many, and this is responsible for the Almshouses in the Cathedral Close in Bangor.

As Archdeacon I had to attend PCCs or Parish Meetings to discuss on behalf of the Bishop, the closure of a particular Church. This was never a pleasant task but in many cases inevitable because of running costs, dwindling congregations, problems of rural community and more recently a shortage of clergy.

Of course such action is not lightly taken and no one gets any pleasure out of it, but what can be to an Archdeacon a statistic which doesn't add up is to old John Jones the source of spiritual life, and we must approach it with reverence and godly fear.

Day to day legal matters are dealt with by a Diocesan Registrar. The long serving Registrar in my time was Michael Preece, whose knowledge and advice we greatly relied on. We have also been fortunate in the loyalty and friendship of the administrative staff in the Diocesan Office, who were always ready to help me with any difficulty. The recent death of Menai, the Senior Administrative Assistant, came as a serious blow to a happy and successful team.

One of the most, if not *the* most fundamental change during the period of my ministry, was the decision of the Church in Wales to ordain women to the priesthood. Although some find it difficult to accept, there is a substantial majority who have welcomed the move, and without their ordination we would be very hard put to provide regular ministry for many of our parishes.

When a see falls vacant for one reason or another, care for the vacant see devolves upon the Archbishop who in turn normally delegates to a senior cleric in the diocese, usually the Senior

Archdeacon. Except for the functions which belong specifically to the episcopal office the Commissary carries out the functions of the Bishop. This happened twice when I was Archdeacon of Bangor, when Cledan and Barry were Bishops. I was also responsible for the Diocese during that interregnum from August 1992 to the end of January 1993. Very much like the work of an Archdeacon the duties were varied, ranging from checking the Burglar Alarm at Tŷ'r Esgob at 3 o'clock in the morning, to answering about twenty letters a day.

I am still reminded of one experience when I was Archdeacon of Bangor. I was enjoying a cup of tea after a busy afternoon's visiting when the telephone rang. The voice at the other end sounded disturbed and agitated and her story unfolded something like this. She was the new Secretary of a Ladies Dining Club and had been let down by the appointed speaker who had informed her minutes before that due to urgent business he was unable to fulfill the appointment. The poor secretary was in a complete muddle and she begged could I step into the breach and save her bacon. She was so distraught she put the phone down with no more ado, apart from telling me where and when the meeting (dinner) was to be held

So I made my way to the hotel at the appointed time and in the pre-dinner chatter the old dear next to me said, "I'm so looking forward to your talk about ghosts!" and the horrible truth dawned on me. She had failed to distinguish between Elwyn and Aelwyn Roberts and to add to the confusion his companion on ghost hunting expeditions was an Elwyn Roberts. I quickly assured the old lady that I knew nothing about ghosts and gave them all a talk on the work of an Archdeacon. That experience is not easily forgotten as in retirement I still receive many phone calls asking me for advice about ghosts and exorcism!

In June 1996, the Dean at that time, Erwyd Edwards, kindly arranged a Diocesan Eucharist in Bangor Cathedral, to mark the 40th Anniversary of my Ordination to the Priesthood. Bishop Barry preached. This proved to be a memorable service.

Chapter 17

RETIREMENT

Bishop Barry stressed that the above service was not a retirement service, as it had been my intention to retire somewhere around my 70th birthday, but circumstances forced me to amend this.

Parkinson's is a curious old affliction. It is a progressive neurological disorder, named after James Parkinson, a London doctor who first identified it and in 1817 wrote his Essay on the Shaking Palsy. Around one in every 500 people have Parkinson's and approximately 10,000 people are diagnosed every year.

In Parkinson's the body's internal communication system is impaired because a "messenger" substance called dopamine is in short supply. There are three main symptoms – shaking (tremor), stiffness (rigidity) and slowness of movement (bradykinesia), which can affect all daily activities including walking, talking, swallowing and writing. All these symptoms may appear very gradually and in no specific order. Since the symptoms of Parkinson's are due to this shortage of dopamine in the brain, much research has been devoted to ways of replacing, stimulating or substituting the supply of this chemical. At present there is no known cure although there are hopeful signs of a breakthrough. I foresee, however, that the breakthrough may well give rise to many ethical issues.

It was during the summer of 1998 that many problems arising from my illness began to reveal themselves. I became aware of a deterioration which made it impossible for me to give my best to my ministry. With Parkinson's there are what they call on/off periods. At one moment one can move about and have complete control, and in a matter of minutes one can have no control whatsoever. There is a stage also when problems are drug related – when one becomes resistant to the drugs. These are problems which I regarded as an embarrassing nuisance, and usually appear as rather violent swings. They made driving difficult. They made chairing a meeting difficult and they also added to the tiredness that normally accompanies Parkinson's.

With retirement would come the added problem of finding a house that we could call our own, and this had to be near the hospital and Tryfan school. But God works in mysterious ways. We saw "Tre'r Ceiri" in Eithinog which is just up the road from Trefonwys, and after our first visit to see the place, we decided that was the home for us. The following day I was in Ysbyty Gwynedd, suffering from heart problems.

We moved house in August 1999 and I retired officially at the end of September of the same year. The following November, Trevor arranged a service at the Cathedral to mark my retirement. Llinos and Sioned read the lessons and the preacher was Bishop Elect Saunders. Once again this was a very memorable service. Since then I have been admitted three times to Ysbyty Gwynedd due to more drug related problems that eventually caused heart failure. All these problems have resulted in my being very dependant on others.

Since I was ordained, I have served under five Bishops, the much loved Bishop J. C. Jones, Bishop G. O. Williams (later Archbishop of Wales), Bishop Cledan Mears, Bishop Barry Morgan (the present Archbishop of Wales), and Bishop Saunders Davies (the present Bishop of Bangor).

When Cledan became Bishop of Bangor we renewed a partnership which we had enjoyed as members of the staff at Saint Michael's College Llandaff. He had the unenviable task of following the long episcopate of Bishop G. O. Williams but he was up to the task. He and Enid moved to Cardiff when they retired and the friendship continues.

Barry succeeded me as Archdeacon of Merioneth, so there was an opportunity for us both to work together as Archdeacons for Bishop Cledan. Barry was consecrated Bishop of Bangor in

January 1993, and he kindly asked me to preach the sermon at the service in St Asaph Cathedral. (See Appendix). He was clear in his objectives and had the determination to carry them out. I shall be forever grateful to him for his kindness in offering me lifts to many meetings that we were both attending, enabling me to continue my ministry for a little longer, despite my Parkinson's. He and Hilary were very sympathetic to my cause.

Bishop Saunders succeeded Barry at about the time that I was retiring for health reasons. It had been my intention, all being well, to have continued with my duties as Archdeacon until I reached the age of 70. Due to my early retirement, I did not have the chance to actually work with Saunders, but I already knew him as a student, and Cynthia, from Saint Michael's College days. It is good to resume an old friendship and we are extremely grateful to them for their thoughtfulness, kindness and regular visits.

Eiflyn and I are also grateful that for the past two years while being unable to attend Church, we have received Communion regularly from Trevor, (who has recently retired as Dean of Bangor). His wife Chris has often accompanied him on his visit. Recently they went on a Diocesan Mission trip to Uganda. They welcomed a return visit from Bishop John Charles and the Reverend Willey Okelo a few weeks ago and we felt very honoured when they brought their visitors to our home. Occasions such as these are always spiritually uplifting.

The Franciscan link from Llandudno days is now maintained once again as Brother Nathanael, who is Priest in Charge of Llannerch-y-medd in Anglesey, calls regularly to visit me.

As mentioned earlier, my Parkinson's was diagnosed by Dr Lees, at the Middlesex Hospital, London. The journey to London (there and back in one day) became impractical for me, and the time came for me to find a Parkinson's Consultant nearer home. My G.P. at the time was my good friend Dr Elwyn and he arranged that I would become a patient of Dr P. N. Ohri who is an Associate Consultant in Ysbyty Gwynedd, and who specialises in the treatment of Parkinson's Disease at a Clinic in

Eryri Hospital, Caernarfon. He gives me and the family a great deal of support, as does Doctor David Jones, our G.P., who visits me regularly at home. Now that Dr Elwyn is retired, we see far more of him and Ann as friends, and they have proved it true – "a friend in need is a friend indeed".

The problem of suffering is age old, and we are no nearer to a solution today than Job was when he wrestled with the problem. You may have heard the story of the two women in adjoining beds in a maternity hospital, and alongside each bed was a cot. In each cot was a baby, one fit and healthy, the other sickly and ill. And the comment from each mother was, "What have I done to deserve this?" Naturally those who suffer often ask the same question. But my motto is still the same as nineteen years ago. There is no point in moaning about your lot – you just have to get on with it.

Our journeys as a clerical family as outlined above have taken us to varied places. Both grandfathers died at an early age so that the children have never known the joys of having a grandfather. The grandmothers fared better. Eiflyn's mother lived into her 80's while my mother is still alive at the age of 98 years. Llinos qualified as a Doctor at the University of Wales College of Medicine, Cardiff, and is at present a Senior House Doctor at Morriston Hospital, Swansea. Sioned gained First Class Honours in B Mus this July at the University of Wales, Bangor. We are very proud of both.

Eiflyn has been a tower of strength to all of us and without her support the whole show would have collapsed long ago. As my Parkinson's increased its hold she gave up her teaching post as Head of Infants at Llandudno Junction in order to look after me at home. Although she had completed a Degree Course in Education a few years previously (and obtained a 1st in it), she sacrificed her own career for the good of the family and for this she cannot be thanked enough.

It is now nineteen years since that day in Criccieth when I heard the news that I had Parkinson's Disease. Since I retired four years ago, my life has become very different. I am not able to drive, my writing is not nearly as neat as it was and sometimes I am not able to walk. Nevertheless, on good days we try occasionally to visit other sick colleagues. We have become experts at discovering places that are wheelchair friendly. We visit countless Garden Nurseries and our favourite haunts are Llanberis, Red Wharf Bay, Bodnant Gardens, Beaumaris, Bangor Pier, Moel-y-don, Holyhead Promenade, Pentir and Mynydd Llandygái, to name but a few.

As a keen gardener at one time, I now take pleasure in choosing what is to be grown, delegating the work to others and eventually enjoying the produce. Rainy days are taken up with crosswords, writing short articles (for publications such as *Y Llan*), reading, Quiz and Documentary programmes on the Television, listening to Morning Services on the Radio, and just relaxing. We soon discovered that when you suffer from Parkinson's Disease, it is almost impossible to plan from one day to the next. Such a great deal depends on the on/off period and the effect of so many tablets.

It is due to the love and care of my family and friends, and the skill of my doctors, that I am here to tell the tale. Naturally people like myself who are suffering from Parkinson's Disease or a similar illness are likely to have bouts of feeling low. That is when I remember the story about the two mothers in hospital and when I turn to my favourite prayer:

> "God,
> grant me the serenity
> to accept the things I cannot change
> courage to change the things I can
> and wisdom to know the difference."

APPENDIX

When I was Archdeacon of Merioneth, the title suggested that I was Archdeacon of an area called Merioneth, but when I became Archdeacon of Bangor, I quickly realised that many people thought I was an Archdeacon based in the Cathedral in Bangor, especially as I also lived in Bangor during that period. As you may remember Art is not my strong point but an idea of how the Diocese of Bangor functions can be seen in this diagram:

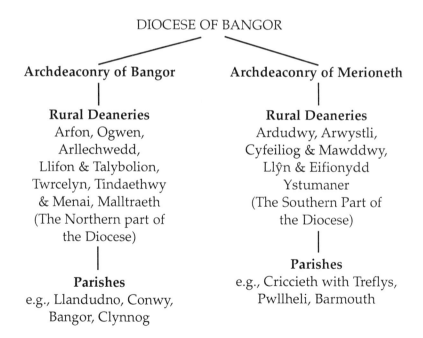

DIOCESE OF BANGOR

Archdeaconry of Bangor

Rural Deaneries
Arfon, Ogwen,
Arllechwedd,
Llifon & Talybolion,
Twrcelyn, Tindaethwy
& Menai, Malltraeth
(The Northern part of
the Diocese)

Parishes
e.g., Llandudno, Conwy,
Bangor, Clynnog

Archdeaconry of Merioneth

Rural Deaneries
Ardudwy, Arwystli,
Cyfeiliog & Mawddwy,
Llŷn & Eifionydd
Ystumaner
(The Southern Part of
the Diocese)

Parishes
e.g., Criccieth with Treflys,
Pwllheli, Barmouth

There are six Dioceses in Wales: Bangor, St Asaph, Swansea and Brecon, St. David's, Monmouth, Llandaff and all six form the ecclesiastical unit of the Province of Wales. Each Diocese has a Bishop and of those six Bishops, one is the Archbishop. There is also an Assistant Bishop for the Province. In addition to the Provincial Committee Meetings, the Governing Body of the Church in Wales meets twice a year. This is a gathering of Representatives, lay and clerical, from each Diocese in the Province.

The Cathedral is the Bishop's Church and is also the Mother Church of the Diocese, where all large Diocesan services are held. Bangor Cathedral founded by Saint Deiniol somewhere around 530 A.D., as well as being the Diocesan Church is also part of the Rectorial Benefice of Bangor along with four other Churches, St Mary's Church, St David's Church, St Peter's Church and Eglwys y Groes, Maesgeirchen.

The Dean is the head of the Cathedral Chapter and together with the Residentiary Canons is responsible for the good order of the Cathedral. Both Archdeacons are also chapter members by virtue of office.

At one time the Precentor was the Canon responsible for the Cathedral music. The Treasurer was the Canon responsible for the finances of the Cathedral. The Cathedral Chancellor was responsible for the educational work of the Cathedral, the two Prebendaries were responsible for part of the finances (Prebend) of the Cathedral.

There used to be four Residentiary Canons who literally took up residence in the Canonry for three months each. Nowadays, chapter members take a token period of duty for one month. There are also Honorary Canons and Minor Canons. A Minor Canon corresponds to a curate in a parish. His duty is to assist with the services in the Cathedral.

Every Cathedral has a Bishop's Chair where the Bishop sits for official Diocesan services. So each Canon has his appointed Stall in the Chancel. There is a Coat of Arms above each Stall and that is the Canon's Stall while he holds office and where he sits for each Diocesan service held in the Cathedral.

Many often ask what is the difference between a Rector and a Vicar. In medieval times the monastery as patron (or Rector) would hold property and send a Vicar to run it on the owner's behalf, but nowadays there is no difference in status. There is provision in the Constitution of the Church in Wales for Rectorial Benefices which is simply an alternative term for team ministry.

In the Bangor Diocese we are fortunate to have many layreaders. These are lay people who are specifically trained to minister in the parishes. In an emergency a Churchwarden is required to conduct a service in the absence of the incumbent. The layreaders are licensed to take services, but are not ordained. Any lay person may be a reader, i.e. one who reads from the scriptures in a service. There is now greater emphasis on lay ministry due to the increase in shortage of clerics.

SERMON PREACHED AT THE CONSECRATION OF THE RIGHT REVD BARRY MORGAN BY THE VENERABLE ELWYN ROBERTS ON 9th JANUARY 1993 AT ST ASAPH CATHEDRAL

Shepherds are certainly familiar figures in the Bible story. We can think, for instance, of David the shepherd boy who became king of Israel; or Amos, the shepherd of Tekoa, who was called to proclaim the judgement of the Lord on a sinful, disobedient people. And there are the shepherds in the field of Bethlehem, to whom came the angelic message of the Saviour's birth, and who in turn became, in the words of the hymn, "the first apostles of his infant fame".

The Old Testament also often depicts God as the shepherd of Israel, guiding and providing for his people; while the experience of the individual of God's love and care is reflected in Psalm 23 – "The Lord is my shepherd, therefore can I lack nothing."

But the Bible also knows of false shepherds – those who behave as hirelings and not as true shepherds. So Ezekiel speaks to kings of Israel who should have shepherded their people, but instead "you take care of yourselves, and never tend the sheep". While Zechariah complains of the shepherd "who does not help the sheep that are threatened by destruction; nor does he look for the lost, or heal those that are hurt, or feed the survivors".

No doubt this image of the shepherd recalls to many of us a familiar favourite, childhood picture of a shepherd carrying on his shoulder the lost sheep, now safely recovered – a peaceful and comforting scene; but we must beware of being sentimental and romantic in our approach to the work of the shepherd. Now sheep can be dirty, smelly, stubborn, wayward creatures, and looking after them was a constant round of rough and exhausting work, exposed to the burning heat of the day and the bitter cold of the night. As Jacob described it "in the day the drought consumed me and frost by night: and my sleep fled from my eyes".

But shepherding was not simply an exhausting occupation, it was also dangerous. If the shepherd led his flock from place to place in search of fresh pasture he had to be on guard against attack by wild animals, and for protection he usually carried, in addition to his long staff for support and for guiding the sheep, an iron-studded club about 3 feet long as a weapon, the "rod and staff" of Psalm 23.

While for the protection of his flock at night the shepherd would often build a sheepfold – a rough stone enclosure topped with thorn branches to keep out wild beasts. The fold had no gate, only a narrow opening, and the shepherd acted as a human gate by lying across the entrance. No sheep could get out without him knowing, and no wild beast could get in except over his dead body.

Such was the hard, demanding, dangerous life of a shepherd in Bible times, and it is against this background that the words of Jesus we heard read in the Gospel are set: I am the good shepherd.

Dengys y Testament Newydd fod pob gweinidogaeth yn yr eglwys yn deillio o berson a gwaith Crist ei hun. Pan ymddangosodd i'w ddisgyblion wedi'r Atgyfodiad rhoddodd iddynt gomisiwn sydd yn cysylltu eu gweinidogaeth hwy â'i weinidogaeth ef – "megis yr anfonodd y Tad fi, felly yr anfonaf fi chwi" – a rhaid felly i'n gweinidogaeth ni adlewyrchu a rhannu natur gweinidogaeth Crist ei hun. Fel y clywsom yn yr Efengyl mae'n disgrifio'r weinidogaeth honno dan ffigwr Bugail Da.

Now I want to suggest two simple thoughts arising out of this very rich image of the shepherd. And the first is the personal love and care of the Good Shepherd for his sheep – "I know my own and my own know me." This is reflected in the Archbishop's charge to the new bishop a little later in this service – "after the example of the chief shepherd you are to know the flock and to be known by them".

Part of the tragedy of our busy, cluttered lives today is that we have too impersonal an approach to life, and the sense of being isolated and alone in an impersonal community is the sad experience of many.

If we are to have any missionary sense at all we must first have a message, a message which is relevant and meaningful to those whom we address. It must be more than "come to church"; more than a general idea that a good dose of Christianity will reduce the crime rate and do people good. These are secondary things. What is primary and fundamental is that something has been done for the world that makes life different from what it would otherwise be: that the Good Shepherd, who knows his own by name, has given his life for the sheep. A modern hymn contains this couplet –

"Life is great if someone loves me
Holds my hand and calls my name."

And the heart of the Gospel is that God does just that – it tells us that we are loved and wanted, however unlovable we may be.

Felly tystion ydym i'r Bugail Da sydd yn rhoddi ei einioes dros y defaid: Y bugail sydd hefyd yn oen yr aberth.

So, Barry, the symbol of your service as bishop may be the shepherd's crook, but the secret of that service must be the Saviour's Cross.

And the second thought is this – the personal attraction of the Good Shepherd for his sheep.

Archbishop William Temple in his *Readings in St. John's Gospel* points out that the Greek word kalos here translated 'good' emphasises that attractive quality of the shepherd's goodness, so he translates "I am the shepherd beautiful". There is a goodness according to the law – but that is not the goodness of the Good Shepherd. His goodness is warm and winsome and attractive.

In one of his writings Bishop Timothy Rees, who was Bishop of Llandaff in the 1930s, tells a story of a parish mission which was a regular instrument of evangelism earlier this century. And at one of the opening meetings the missioner asked a group of children a question, a standard question to which there was a standard answer, rather like a Catechism. The question was "What is a mission for?"; and the expected answer – "To make bad people good, and good people better."

After a forest of hands shot up the missioner pointed to one little girl – "Now tell us", he said, "what is a mission for?" To which the little girl replied – "A mission is to make bad people good, and good people nice". And Bishop Timothy wryly comments – "A vast improvement on the expected answer!"

And George Sangster, a noted Methodist preacher, is said to have once told his congregation – with more guts than I've got – "My friends, do you realise that some people are not in church this morning because you are". Yes , there is a goodness which can be cold and off-putting and even repulsive.

Oes, mae yna fath ar ddaioni sydd yn oeraidd ac annymunol, cyfiawnder sydd yn ôl y ddeddf. Ond nid dyna gyfiawnder y bugail da. Mae'r daioni hwn yn hawddgar a phrydferth – ac o'r herwydd yn atyniadol.

But the Good Shepherd is not one who looks after sheep with cold efficiency – he tends them with a sacrificed love. When the sheep are in trouble, he doesn't nicely calculate the risks of helping them – he gives his life for the sheep. The Good Shepherd is the shepherd whose service is a lovely and winsome thing because it is a service, rendered for love and in love.

Mae yna warant i ni yn y Testament Newydd i edrych ar Iesu fel ein hesiampl a'n patrwm. Cofiwn, er enghraifft, am y ddameg a'r weithred honno ar noson y Swper olaf pan gyfododd oddi wrth y bwrdd ac a gymerodd dywel, ac a aeth o amgylch gan olchi traed ei ddisgyblion. Ac wedi iddo eistedd dywedodd wrthynt, "Nid yw gwas yn fwy na'i feistr . . . yr wyf fi wedi rhoi esiampl i chwi: yr ydych chwithau i wneud yn union fel yr wyf i wedi gwneud i chwi".

The New Testament gives us warrant for thinking of Christ as our pattern and example – but by itself the thought of Christ as our example will not carry us very far. Indeed it will lead us only to despair, for the standards of the Good Shepherd will be far beyond our reach. But he is not just our example – He is the Lord who has done something for us and in us, by which we find ourselves in a new situation. His life is not there to mock us, but is a dynamic pattern, a power house from which we may draw and so grow more and more into his likeness.

So, we commend Barry to God with the prayer that as people come to know him they will find in fact another, who is in truth the Lord, the Good Shepherd, who died for us and who lives and reigns for evermore.